RIPLEY'S
VERY ROUGH GUIDE TO
RUGBY

RIPLEY'S
VERY ROUGH GUIDE TO
RUGBY

ANDY RIPLEY
and Geoff Atkinson

Illustrations by Borin van Loon

Stanley Paul
London Sydney Auckland Johannesburg

Stanley Paul and Co. Ltd

An imprint of Century Hutchinson

Brookmount House, 62-65 Chandos Place,
Covent Garden, London WC2N 4NW

Century Hutchinson Australia (Pty) Ltd
20 Alfred Street, Milsons Point, Sydney 2061, Australia

Century Hutchinson New Zealand Limited
191 Archers Road, PO Box 40-086, Glenfield, Auckland 10

Century Hutchinson South Africa (Pty) Ltd
PO Box 337, Bergvlei 2012, South Africa

First published 1989
Copyright © Andy Ripley and Geoff Atkinson, 1989

Set in Plantin by SX Composing Limited

Printed and bound in Great Britain by
Butler & Tanner Ltd, Frome and London

British Library Cataloguing in Publication Data
Ripley, Andy
Ripley's very rough guide to rugby.
1. Rugby football
I. Title
796.33'3

ISBN 0 09 174072 X

Original photography by Yeofi Andoh

CONTENTS

FOREWORD

By Mrs Andy Ripley

I would like to welcome you to this book by my husband. Unfortunately I know very little indeed about rugby myself, apart from the few bits and pieces Andy has explained, and so the book is rather lost on me, although Andy tells me it is very good so I suppose it must be.

Actually that isn't quite true; there was one joke I did get on page 52. Or was it page 53? Or was it that page with all the photographs on? Anyway, I thought it was quite funny at the time, after Andy had explained it to me, although I can't quite remember what it was now. Oh yes, and I thought one of the little drawings was quite funny too. Although when Andy explained it to me it didn't seem quite as funny as I'd first thought because I'd read it to mean something completely different and nothing at all to do with rugby.

Oh, and there was one other bit I quite liked as well. Although I can't remember what that was either. I think it was either the bit about ladies' rugby or the bit about track-suits, or was it something else? Oh dear, I can't remember; well, look, I definitely remember it was towards the back of the book just after the bit I was reading when the man came to read the electricity meter.

Anyway, the thing is, if you like rugby then I'm sure this is just the book for you because one of Andy's rugby friends came round last night and he read it and laughed a lot and he doesn't usually laugh at anything. And someone else who came round the other day had a flick through and said they liked it and asked me if I'd read the bit on rugby tactics and started to quote a bit that didn't mean anything to me but which they certainly seemed to find very funny indeed.

Anyway, I hope you like the book and on behalf of Andy may I wish you all happy reading.

Mrs Andy Ripley
(Oh hang about, I've just flicked through the book and I think that funny joke I was trying to remember was on page 32, although now I look at it again it isn't quite as funny as I remembered.)

Andy Ripley *is a former England International who was capped 24 times for his country and is a legend of the rugby field where his performances for Rosslyn Park and for the British Lions have made him into one of the game's most loved and respected statesmen.*

Geoffrey Atkinson *isn't.*

INTRODUCTION

Hi, and welcome to **Ripley's Very Rough Guide to Rugby**, the definitive guide to the new three Rs!

For many years I have been courted by the press, begged to tell my story, enticed to rip the lid off my outrageous and hellraiser life and tell the hot and stormy truth. Yet I have resisted. Until now.

Now at last, with my boots finally hung up, and my fortieth birthday but a memory (well actually, it's a collection of polaroids in a Boots photo album) – now at last I am prepared to tell all!

This is my red hot raunchy story that will blow the rugby world wide open. The story they said could never be told. The story they said would never be told. But now I'm telling it to you, first, here in this exclusive book! It is torrid, it is unbelievable, it is a story that sizzles with sensation and which I guarantee you won't be able to put down!

And you can only read it here, in this book. The unexpurgated saga a whole nation has been waiting to hear. Now at last I am prepared to unlock the lid on the stories you have been begging me to tell.

It's outrageous! It's sensational! It's Ripley's Very Rough Guide to Rugby.

Read it if you dare!!!!!!

Andy Ripley
(Actually, it's just a personal collection of pieces
about rugby, but the publishers said it would read a
bit flat if I said that – Andy)

I

THE ORIGINS OF THE GAME

Through the ages

It is wrongly claimed in the textbooks that the game of rugby originated at Rugby School some time in the last two hundred years.

We now know for a fact that the game's roots are much earlier and almost certainly not from this country or even this continent but were probably from the Far East.

It seems that as long ago as the twelfth century the roots of the modern game were seeded in the ancient sport of 'Sa Nin Yat Suki' (literally 'the Sa that Nin's or Yat's a Suki').

In this sport a person would pick up one of his opponents and run with him in his arms while pursued by his opponents. Those running the furthest were awarded a Yensenko (or a 'yensenko'). In time, players stopped picking up other players and instead picked up other players' wives and ran off with them. This didn't improve the game although the players seemed to enjoy it more and it paved the way for the sixties' phenomena of wife swapping.

Finally, towards the fourteenth century, the game took another change as players started picking up other players' property and running off with that. It was at this point that the armlock and the full body tackle appeared in the game and the sport began to take its present form.

Gradually over the next two hundred years a ball (or 'ball' as it would be called) seems to have made its appearance and players would attempt to run off with this. Thus the game was born.

But it was still far from its present form and was to undergo many changes before it at last arrived on Western shores.

For a period it was popular on the island of Honshu in Japan where a kamikaze form was introduced. Players would attempt to run with the ball but upon being stopped would collapse upon their swords in disgrace. Faced with the appalling death rate, many switched over to Sumo Rugby where huge great human puddings would chase after one another in loincloths, any tackle resembling not so much an athletic act but more the coming together of two giant blancmanges.

Later, back on mainland China, Samurai Rugby, played out between teams of ten thousand sword-wielding opponents caused immense bloodshed and a temporary stop to the game; while on stage Chinese ballet reflected the public's interest in the sport with

The new face of South African rugby (artist's impression)

the first performance of the hitherto little seen ballet 'Madame Butterfly-half'.

Meanwhile in Mongol China the sport of Rogha Be was becoming popular as tribesmen used a cow, and later a cow's bladder, as a makeshift ball.

Finally, in Southern Manchuria the game evolved into a more recognisable form with two teams competing over a simple marked surface. It was crude, primitive, and had little refinement or form, although it is curious that the complicated offside ruling was almost identical to its present day form.

The evolution of the ball

How did the rugby ball come to be shaped as it is? The most likely answer is that Thomas Arnold, the then headmaster of Rugby School, on deciding to invent a game for his pupils determined that it should be a game like no other. Consequently he set about identifying as many different ways as possible that his game would be unique. He saw the football goals and added extra length to the upright. He studied other sports and discovered that none had fifteen players per team so he at once chose that for his game. He spotted that every other sport had a round ball so at once he hit upon the novel idea of making his version hyperbolic.

But what are less well known are the other changes that Arnold was keen to employ but later dropped as too fanciful.

Arnold's unadopted rules for rugby:

1 All players to wear frilly little skirts.
2 Only players with one leg to be allowed to take part if the game takes place on a Thursday or the second Tuesday in March.
3 Live chickens to be used as the ball in selected games.
4 Referees to be equipped with a trombone instead of a whistle.
5 Disputed tries to be settled by a pistol duel.
6 The game to last for two equal halves of thirty-eight years.
7 Players to be allowed to place live goldfish down their shorts if they so wish.
8 The goalposts to be made out of cheese.

As an experiment a game employing the adopted rules was played in 1975. It was not a success.

Different types of players

Rugby used to be a simple sport. You turned up. You played the game. You got drunk afterwards. You went home. And that, basically, was it. Except for those players who turned up, didn't play but still got drunk. All players were the same and differed only in how well they played and the amount of drink they could consume.

Nowadays it is a much changed sport. Of course there is still the diehard traditionalist who gets smashed to bits on the field and smashed to bits off it. But rugby has moved with the times and a new breed of player who is likely to scorn his predecessors' ways is fast coming to the fore.

Cleanest of the clean is the would-be international. He is aware of fitness, aware of body care, aware of diet. He is likely to jog straight from the match to the training field for further coaching. From there he will jog to the gym for a further workout before retiring home for a full night's sleep and more training. If pressed, he will accept an orange juice (preferably fresh). He commands respect and admiration for his self restraint, but deep down we cannot in our hearts see that it is worth the effort.

Next in line comes the family man. He is likely to have a wife, children, a mortgage and obligations. He would like to stay after the game but has promised to get back because there are people coming round for dinner. He will turn up for the game in a state of confusion having done the shopping, picked up the kids, repaired the back gate, and hung the laundry out, all before he arrived. During the game his mind will be elsewhere, and he will miss a vital catch when his wife and kids arrive midway through the second half and start waving at him from the touchline. The great sadness is that deep down he wants to be one of the lads again but he, and we, know he is a lost cause.

Then there are the young pretenders. Rugby has attracted a new wave of players over the last few years. Young, smartly dressed, flash even, they are often defectors from football and bring with them the footballers' ways. For a start they will blow dry their hair after a game. Unheard of by the old regime. They will use after shave and deodorant. And dry thoroughly before they dress. And while they might stop for a swift half of lager in the clubhouse after the game they will as likely hop into their 'wheels' and hot foot it down to the local disco on the make. A jolly night singing rugby songs and balancing beer mugs on their heads is not for them.

Finally, we come to the old pretenders, the diehards who stick to their old ways. The trouble is with so many absentees the spirit of the post-match booze up is largely crushed. Where twenty louts could revel in their joint mayhem four or five middle-aged gents led by Crampo de Gambo with pot-bellies and grey hair cannot conjure up the same excitement, and merely conjure up a great deal of embarrassment.

In short, the game has changed and it is no good crying into one's beer. But for those still insistent on the old ways the Post-Match Tradition is described in Chapter 9.

2

THE TEAMS

Schools rugby

The advent of mini rugby, discussed later in this chapter, has changed the face of schools rugby, and with the exception of the parents who support it is generally a good thing.

However the full-size game still struggles on, at least in the public-school sector, though not without its critics. The problem is that even at the most junior level the game is still commonly played to adult conventions on a full-size pitch with regulation ball and posts. Schoolboys half the size of their adult counterparts must play a game designed for players twice their size. It is like asking an adult player to run 250 yards with a two-feet high ball before touching down and making a 70-yard conversion kick over a crossbar twenty feet high.

Add to this the differing development of boys through adolescence where an early developed 14-stoner may play alongside a six-stone late developer and the problems become acute.

It is little wonder that among the compulsory junior house and Saturday morning teams there is a rich vein of boys who have no interest in the game and who spend the greater part of any match trying to get as far away as possible from the ball.

Whole games are spent with both teams running away from each other as fast as possible while passes, when they are unavoidable, are made by briefly pulling both hands from the trouser pockets before shoving them back again to keep warm. The ritual is complicated still further by enthusiastic games masters, keen to inject an enthusiasm for the game and shouting for the shivering bystanders to get stuck in.

Indeed, in many games the master in charge takes the whole matter a stage further by fielding the ball himself and acting as a part-time player for both sides. Intercepting a pass, he will spot a player from the opposing side counting buttercups on the far touchline and heave a pass to him, only to intervene a few seconds later to reverse the play with a pass to a shrinking player on the original team.

Since he holds the whistle he can continue to run things in a way that destroys even the last semblance of a match. To watch a game like this is alarming. In adult games, the referee plays an active part but not to the point of directing play, fielding the ball, and taking part as unofficial sixteenth man to both sides. Even into later life players exposed to this form of schooling suffer severe neurosis and will on occasion slip a pass to the referee, their days playing alongside the domineering influence of 'sir' having left a telling mark.

Rugby at sea

Deck rugby is a cross between quoits and conventional rugby. Heavy rubber rings or discs are thrown on to a marked court (as for the game of quoits); after which you attempt to throw your opponents after them (as for rugby). Sometimes the discs themselves are omitted and players simply throw each other. On other occasions, the court is omitted and players attempt to throw each other over the side of the ship. This is not really a kind of rugby, more a form of loutish behaviour that takes place on the sea crossings of foreign tours.

A form of deck rugby based on the sevens game has been developed for use on larger liners, though never put into practice. The game was intended for the ballroom area and worked on a reduced size pitch and close passing. While it was considered operable in calm weather it was felt that in heavy seas with a 20-degree list players might be unable to keep their feet and might present a serious danger to themselves and others – an odd interpretation since much of the game of rugger is based on the very premise that this is the case.

Mini rugby

One of the phenomenal growth areas of the modern game has been mini rugby. This is a variant form of the normal game developed to foster an interest in the game in school and pre-school children.

Mini rugby is similar to normal rugby but with a number of important changes:

1 Mini rugby matters more than ordinary rugby.
2 Mini rugby matters more than international rugby.
3 Mini rugby matters more than life and death.

Right: Youngsters should be trained to play the game as robustly as possible

Such is the fever with which spectators and players become involved that many life assurance companies now have a clause excluding all mini rugby fans from making claims.

One of the notable aspects of the game is the age at which players can now start to play.

Above left: Increase conversion run up distance in inverse proportion to the person's size. Thus a person half full adult size should double the run up distance. In this case the kicker is taking a 72 yard run up to counter his lack of inches

Above right: Where lack of height is a problem try doubling up to reduce any deficit

YOUNGSTERS' ACTIVITY PLAN

Years

0–1   Cannot actually pass or kick a ball but can be encouraged to practise full body lock tackles on his/her teddy bear.

1–3   Should be taught the principal rules of the game. (A good trick is to weave them into some existing story book. Postman Pat could suddenly find himself making a reverse loop pass with one of his mail bags, etc. Super Ted might be caught in possession on his own goalline and be forced to kick into touch rather than risk calling for the mark.) By age three should know more about the game than Bill McLaren.

4–6   By the time he/she is six, the average rugby-induced child should be able to set up a seven-player move, which can sweep sixty yards across the playground and expose the weakness at wing threequarters in their opponents' line-up that a diagonal cross pass might open up. Minimum of three hours' rugby practice a night.

Over 6   Should be able to take part in an adult game. And win most of the balls against the head.

Aged 8   Think about retirement from the game.

Mixed rugby

Mixed rugby – unlike club rugby, county rugby, women's rugby, mini rugby, rugby sevens or any other type of rugby come to that – is alone in being the only form of the game taken seriously by absolutely no-one.

It exists only for two reasons:

1   As an important and extremely laudable sponsored event that can, and indeed often does, raise considerable sums for charity.
2   As a blatant and obvious excuse for women to grab hold of men's testicles.

The latter is obviously the more important of the two, though perhaps requires a little elaboration.

Despite the increasing scorn placed on sexist behaviour in the last few years, chauvinism of the MCP variety is still all too prevalent. A man may pinch a woman's bottom or otherwise molest her with little or no thought of retribution. Indeed, sadly, it is very often seen as a mark of prowess. By contrast, there are few occasions when women may get their own back – except on the rugby field. For it is here, in a contact sport, that women may at last legitimately enjoy the ideal opportunity to repay all those years of groping and molestation they have been made to suffer. In short, the perfect chance to return the compliment.

It is little wonder then that given such a release valve women should take it, literally, in both hands. It is as though a thousand years of frustration have been released in an instance, or rather in eighty minutes.

Not only that, few women appreciate the pain such 'tackling' can inflict, in much the

Most top players would prefer a season of this to twenty minutes of mixed rugby

same way that most men fail to appreciate the emotional scarring their own actions inflict. Indeed, not only do most women fail to appreciate the risks, they also fail to let go once the damage is done, playfully hanging on till grim death with a shrill, gleeful cry of 'I've caught one here, girls!' As a result, many men are left quite unable to walk for weeks after such a contest.

Worse still, the injury toll is increased dra-matically by the failure of most players to take elementary precautions. Few men consider wearing jock straps in a mixed game, wrongly assuming they will face none of the risks of a conventional battle.

For this reason seasoned mixed rugby players view it with more fear than a full-blooded encounter in the local division. While they may sleep soundly before a vital crunch match with their arch rivals, a Sunday morning romp with the local nurses' hostel may cause them to spend many a sleepless night racked with anxious worry and trepida-tion.

London teams

Exiled teams in London have always enjoyed popular support. London Irish, London Scottish and London Welsh have large and loyal followings that keep their national support alive in the metropolis.

As the capital becomes increasingly cosmopolitan newer national groupings are finding it possible to organise ex-pat teams. Among those with enthusiastic support are:

London Isle Of Wight
London Albanian
London Pitcairn Islands
London Antarctica
London London   (for all ex-Londoners now living in London)
London London London London   (for all Londoners living in London who like to play for a team with a very very very silly name)
London London London London London London London   (as above, except for people who don't know when the joke has gone on too long)
London Welsh Algerian Peru   (for Welsh-Algerians living in London with at least one Peruvian parent)
London Welsh Algerian Peru New Guinea   (for Welsh-Algerians living in London with at least one Peruvian parent and a New Guinean half-cousin)
London Welsh Algerian Peru New Guinea Luxembourg   (for Welsh-Algerians living in London with at least one Peruvian parent and a New Guinean half-cousin of Luxembourgi extraction) [operates six teams in the London Home Counties League]
London, A to Z   (see London street maps)
London, Brian   (see boxing)
London, Streets of   (see music)
London Underground
London Rockall
London Irish-Scottish-Welsh (takes any player of very confused parentage)
London illegitimate   (takes any player of no fixed parentage)

Gypsy teams

If one law has been learnt from my years in rugby, it is never to play against a gypsy team. This advice emanates not from the fear that a gypsy curse may be laid against the whole team but rather from the simple impracticalities of a fixture of this kind.

For if the ordinary player is dogged by superstition, and has an armful of bizarre personal rituals he/she must obey, then the gypsy team is quite simply riddled with them.

A player may need to dress and undress for several hours in order that he doesn't break some gypsy custom. The ribbing of the socks may need to be minutely adjusted in front of the mirror for ages, or a special fairy potion sprinkled over the dressing-room floor to bless the players' feet who tread in it.

At the very best, it may well take a gypsy team several hours to get to the point where they are ready to take the pitch and even then it may prove impossible since all fifteen players like to emerge at number nine in the line and thus find it quite impossible to squeeze down the tunnel in a line fifteen men abreast.

Meanwhile you have been waiting patiently on the pitch watching the shadows lengthen and trying to work out why your wing threequarters has just turned into a giant toad.

Countries to play

While it is not possible to avoid mismatches, it is generally possible to load them in your favour by arranging fixtures against second or third or seventh class rugby nations. Fixtures in the following countries are more likely to produce a mismatch in your favour:

Peru
Guatamala
Tibet
Andorra
Chad
Nepal
Upper Volta
Lower Volta
Upper Lower Volta

Lower Upper Volta
Upper Lower Upper Volta
Lower Upper Lower Uppa Volta
Upper Lower Upper Lower Lower Upper
  Upper Lower Volta*
Rutland
Togoland
Toyland
Legoland
Iceland
China
Antarctica
Never Never Land

*For a full list of potential opponents in the Volta see the special Volta supplement supplied free with all Volta editions of this book.

Rugby sevens

Rugby sevens came about from a desire to add new interest to the game. It was agreed that a change in numbers might be one way of adding new colour to the game and the question was raised of what the new figure should be.

One thought was to extend the size of the team and a serious plan for rugby forty-fives was on the cards for some time. The advantage of this was that three matches could take place where only one had previously been possible and valuable pitch space could be sold off for lucrative re-development. The negative to this was a game that was impossible to follow and which had little or no flow,

soon becoming a muddy pitched battle that looked more like some trench encounter from the First World War. Eventually the idea was tossed out and while other figures were mentioned (36, 71, 23, 167), none was found suitable.

It was then agreed that a reduction in numbers might be more sensible and a figure less than fifteen sought. Here again the extremists soon put in a strong case for one-man rugby. Early trials proved the idea unworkable: after five minutes, both players were shattered; after ten, they were calling for a doctor; and after fifteen, they had collapsed in the middle and settled for an honourable draw.

It was at this stage that the novel idea of halving the playing strength was muted and the concept of rugby seven-and-a-halves came to be mentioned. Early euphoria was somewhat dampened when it was realised that the half might present a problem. Various solutions were offered: perhaps a one-legged player would count as the half; or maybe a midget could be employed. One promising idea was that one player should play half-heartedly, and this seemed a profitable possibility until it was realised the other seven members of the team were likely to be no different.

Other thoughts were that the half player could be one player representing both sides simultaneously and that for half the time he should run the ball one way, and for the other half he should run it the opposite way. Or that he could only play in half the field and must pull up sharp immediately he reached the halfway line.

In the end though all these solutions were dismissed and for the sake of simplicity the seven and a half was rounded down to seven in order that it might come to fruition. (In certain cannibal communities a form of variable-a-side is practised where the number of players on the pitch at any one time varies according to the number that have been eaten. Not to be confused with the Eton/Harrow game which is a game between Eton and Harrow schools and has nothing at all to do with cannibalism.)

Indoor rugby

When the weather proves too stiff for a game, and in the world of rugby a force ten gale and a fifty mile an hour hurricane still only count as a squally shower, but when the weather really does become impossible a neat solution is to try a game of indoor rugby. Already tennis, cricket and football have all adapted suitably to indoor formats so it is natural that the long ball game has followed suit.

The game is played along similar lines to the conventional game with one or two differences, the principal one being that tackles are made by 'tigging' the opponent and not by bringing him to the ground.

The problem with this is that it eliminates from the game that most important of features – unwanted aggression – and reduces it down to the vapour of a timid parlour game. For this reason a number of solutions are offered:

1 Inclusion of a separate 'tackle room'.

The referee would tot up the total number of 'tigs' made by each side during the match then at the end of the game each team would be allotted that number of 'free' assaults on an opponent of their choice. The tackle room would have a mud floor and soundproofed walls. As a bonus, players might be able to raise extra money by paying to commit extra tackles.

2 Tigging by a boxing glove.
Players would still tig in the conventional way but would be allowed to strike the opponent with a gloved fist. This would reduce the dangers of injury from an artificial surface that indoor rugby brings, without reducing the carnage.

3 By re-defining the term 'tig' and allowing it to include the act of grabbing the opponent by both ankles and wrestling him to the ground.

4 By all the above.

Pro-celebrity rugby

One interesting development over recent years has been the growth in popularity of pro-celebrity rugby, in which established teams take on famous personalities from the show business and entertainment fields. Among early fixtures suggested have been:

Bonnie Langford v P Ringer

A J P Taylor v The Combined Universities' Pack

Fiona Fullerton v The Barbarians' Pack

Keith Harris & Orville v The All Blacks .

Playing for England

One of the greatest thrills an English player can experience is his England call-up. Few players forget their first cap. But few supporters realise the amount of hard work it involves. Not just on the pitch and training ground, but behind the scenes too. The days after a call-up are full of fittings and measurements and visits to the England clothiers. Nothing is left to chance in the England player's wardrobe. For, as well as his cap, the following items of clothing are all issued by the rugby authorities:

England blazer
England tie
England vest
England underpants (1 pr coral, 1 pr plain)
England socks
England hairbrush
England pyjama case
England shoelaces (2)
England plastic raincoat

England beenie hat
England comb
England thigh-length fisherman's waders
England surgical support garment
England kipper tie (discounted 1978)
England pantie girdle (issued on request)
England G-string (issued on request)
England flip-flops
England pompom slippers
England duffle bag

England players are expected to keep their England 'kit' in full repair and on tour there is a daily kit inspection at 8 a.m. every morning.

Caps

All the national squads issue caps to their players except France who issue a beret and Australia who issue a hat with corks attached.

More playing for England

Apart from turning out on a Saturday for club games, divisional games, charity games, Public School Wanderers' games, and county games, the average international player is expected to supplement his four games per Saturday with training on at least eight nights a week, regular coaching sessions for the colts, and extra road training, before, after, and, if possible, during work. Saturday games are followed by four obligatory press interviews, six less obligatory interviews, and a grilling by the cub reporter from the local free sheet who hasn't taken shorthand and has to write every quote down in longhand.

This is generally followed by seven after-dinner speeches, fourteen replies to the visiting Captain's speech and a round of toasts for everyone from the host groundsman to the tea lady's sister's half-cousin. For all of this he receives not a single penny for his services, and indeed he must even stump up a five pound fifty supplement on the hotel bill because his girlfriend had breakfast on the morning after the Wallabies' game.

An international player is expected to have a diary that covers fourteen months a year, nine days a week, twenty-seven hours a day, and twelve years in a decade. And when he is not playing, talking or discussing rugby, he is expected to read or write or commentate on the game.

For this reason international players invariably seek out employment that supports them in their sleepless lifestyle.

Top among the jobs is any career that is both self-employed and highly remunerative. Any job that can support fifty-one weeks of rugby with one week of toil is ideal. Failing this a job in teaching is a very good second best.

Other proposed careers for the would-be internationalist are:

- **Male model**
  Often only half an hour's work a week required and physically undemanding.

- **Pope**
  Initially not promising, but remember you are your own boss so there's no-one above you to tell you what to do, plus you can work your own hours.

- **Understudy in a West End show**
  If you're lucky you might never need to go on which means you earn a decent wage without having to raise a finger. Especially good are shows understudying Michael Crawford who goes on no matter what so you can practically guarantee a cushy life. Remember, you'll have to make the show every night plus a Saturday matinee, which could be a bit tricky. When you apply for the job see if they're prepared to employ a second understudy to act as your understudy for performances that clash with rugby fixtures.

- **Astronaut**
  Most astronauts only spend a few days up in the sky in their whole life, so you'll have weeks and weeks free to play rugby. Remember, if you are picked to play rugby while you're in space on a mission then you will normally not be allowed to pop back home for the game.

- **Criminal**
  The average criminal spends only a few minutes carrying out any crime. A typical bank raid may take less than three minutes, and even allowing for swapping cars, getting rid of the weapons, and fixing up an alibi, it isn't going to take you more than a few hours. Yet in that time you can earn enough to support you as a player for several years, if you pick the right job. Remember if you are caught you won't be able to play for your club or country, but you might get the occasional run out with the prison team.

- **Bimbo**
  Many Bimbos lead an exciting and profitable life without going to work. The trick is to secure some rich sugar daddy who will support you. This isn't easy. Few rugby players make good pin-ups and even with make-up and stilettos they fall far short of the normal quality of Bimbo found at Tramps and Stringfellows. Nevertheless, fortune never favoured the faint-hearted and although it is a long shot it is worth a gamble if the other ploys fail to work. Do remember to shave your arms and legs before you go out. And do make sure you do this privately. Shaving body hair publicly with the rest of the team may arouse suspicion. And do watch out for the paparazzi. It may seem a laugh to have the story of how the bass guitarist of the Rolling Stones is making a fool of himself over you spread across all the papers but it won't do much for your international rugby prospects.

- **SDP Party Chairman**
  The ideal part-time job. You should be

able to get through the work in half a morning which leaves the rest of the week free for rugby.

- **Captain of the British women's lawn tennis team**
One day a month should be enough; ideal for would-be rugby internationalists.

- **Russian undercover agent**
Most undercover agents have a straight job to conceal their true identity. In fact it is a specific requirement with most spying appointments. And what better cover than an international rugby player? Do be careful to warn your contacts of your rugby commitments or they may try and make contact with you during a vital game. There is nothing more embarrassing than a strange head appearing next to yours in the scrum and starting to jabber excitedly in Russian.

- **Semi-retired multi-millionaire business person**
The secret of becoming a rich business person is to do something that earns you lots and lots of money which you can put in the bank to make even more money. Once you have earned lots of money you can sit around and do anything you want.

Sharing a room

One of the great mysteries of International Rugby that I never fathomed in all my years in the game is the need for players to share hotel rooms on away fixtures. This is a custom that persists to this day with all five nations yet few, if any, are sure why.

One reason put forward is the feeling of teamship and camaraderie that sleeping together brings. This is pure hokum. There can be little friendship gained from sharing a bed with a man who snores half the night and pinches all the bedclothes.

The second reason offered is that it gives re-assurance and helps to settle jangling nerves on the eve of an important match. Again this must be a patent falsehood. Surely a player who is about to go out and do battle in front of sixty thousand frenzied rugby fans the following afternoon cannot be in such a state of nervous terror that he is too scared to go to sleep alone.

The third reason often given is that it helps players to get to know one another and bond a spirit of togetherness, though knowing what colour pyjamas a fellow player wears, or whether he squeezes the toothpaste tube from the bottom or top, is surely not instrumental to the tactical cohesion of a rugby team.

No, reluctantly, the reason must be admitted; it is simply that the authorities are looking to save money, and two players to a room is a simple ploy that makes prudent economical sense. Never mind the revenue the game generates, if you don't look after the pennies then the pounds will never look after themselves. And if that means two twenty-stone meat monsters sharing a hotel bedroom together then so be it.

And before a howl of outrage is heard in protest at such mealy mindedness we should perhaps count a few blessings. After all it could be worse. The players could be decamped to some out of town bed and breakfast, or cut-price caravan park, or perhaps a set of tents could be erected outside the ground to cut expenses completely. In future, players could be selected not on their playing abilities but on whether they own their own sleeping bag and how good they are at brewing a pot of tea on a portable primus.

3

TRAINING AND TACTICS

Passing

One of the problems with rugby is the need to pass the ball backwards. The disadvantage of this is the swifter and more proficient a team becomes at releasing the ball the quicker the ball travels backwards down the field towards its own line. Theoretically, if the ball is passed at the breakneck speed encouraged in the training manuals it is quite possible for a team pressing on the opponents' goalline to feed the ball back to their own line without an opponent intervening. Thus they find themselves in a defensive tangle, lending fuel to the theory that slowness and incompetence is in some cases a hidden virtue.

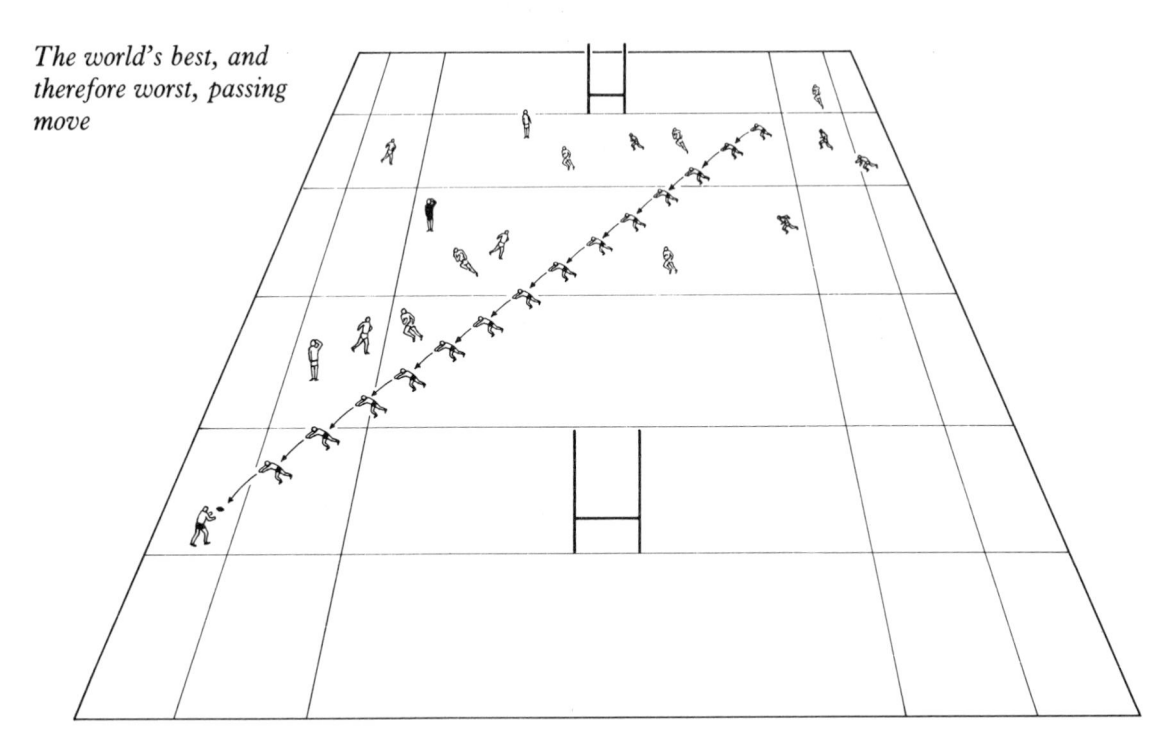

The world's best, and therefore worst, passing move

An improvised defence ploy

Defences often find themselves trapped on their own goalline where it is difficult to move the ball or kick into touch. In these situations it may be more sensible to improvise a strategy. Remember: while you hold the ball you still hold the advantage, and in these situations your opponents will not be expecting exotic or unusual tricks. Below is one possible example.

Player 'A' has used the posts to his advantage to wrong foot his opponents and open up space

dead ball line

goal line

Fitness runs for the less fit

A great deal is written in the rugby press about fitness training for the fit and active player, some of it, indeed, by me. Below I outline a special weekly fitness plan for the less-than-keen player.

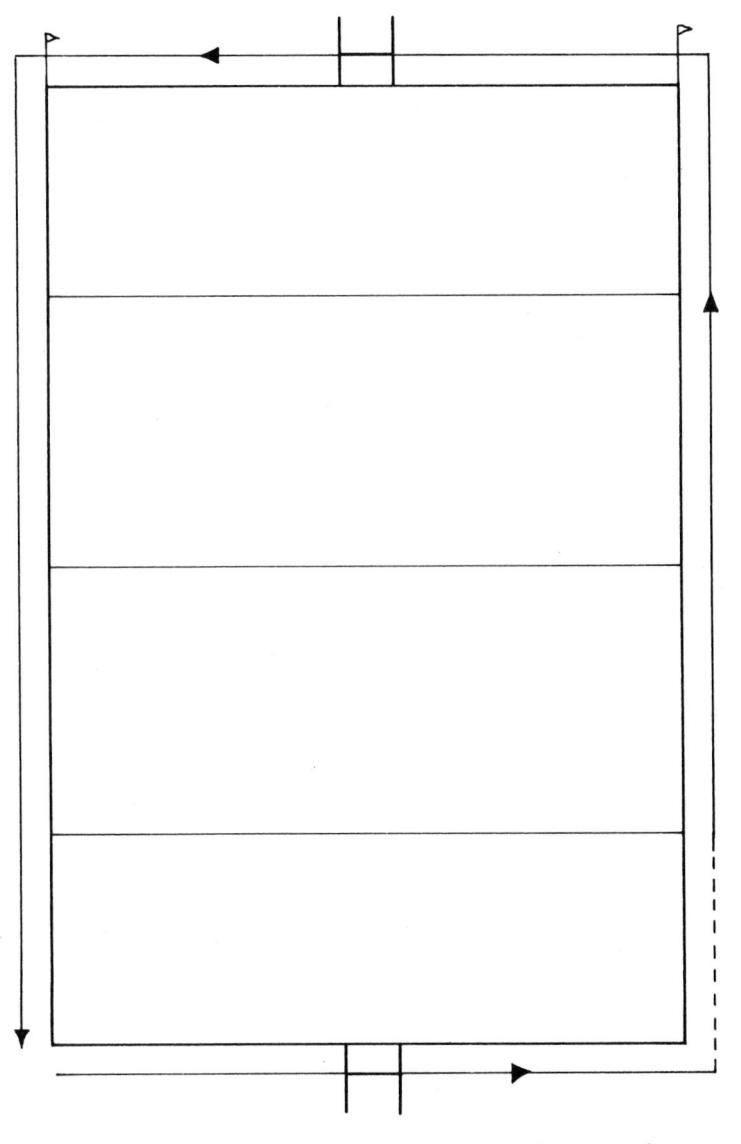

- - - - - - - - ▶ run   *(As an alternative, the run sections may be walked as well)*

———————▶ walk   *(As alternative alternative, the whole thing may be driven in a car)*

Scrumming machines

A useful companion on the training field is the scrumming machine. This allows a team to perfect their scrum technique without the humiliation of training against the Special Extra 'B' and losing.

However scrumming machines aren't always readily available and it may be necessary to seek compromises. Below are a selection of alternatives for the keen pack anxious to improve their technique.

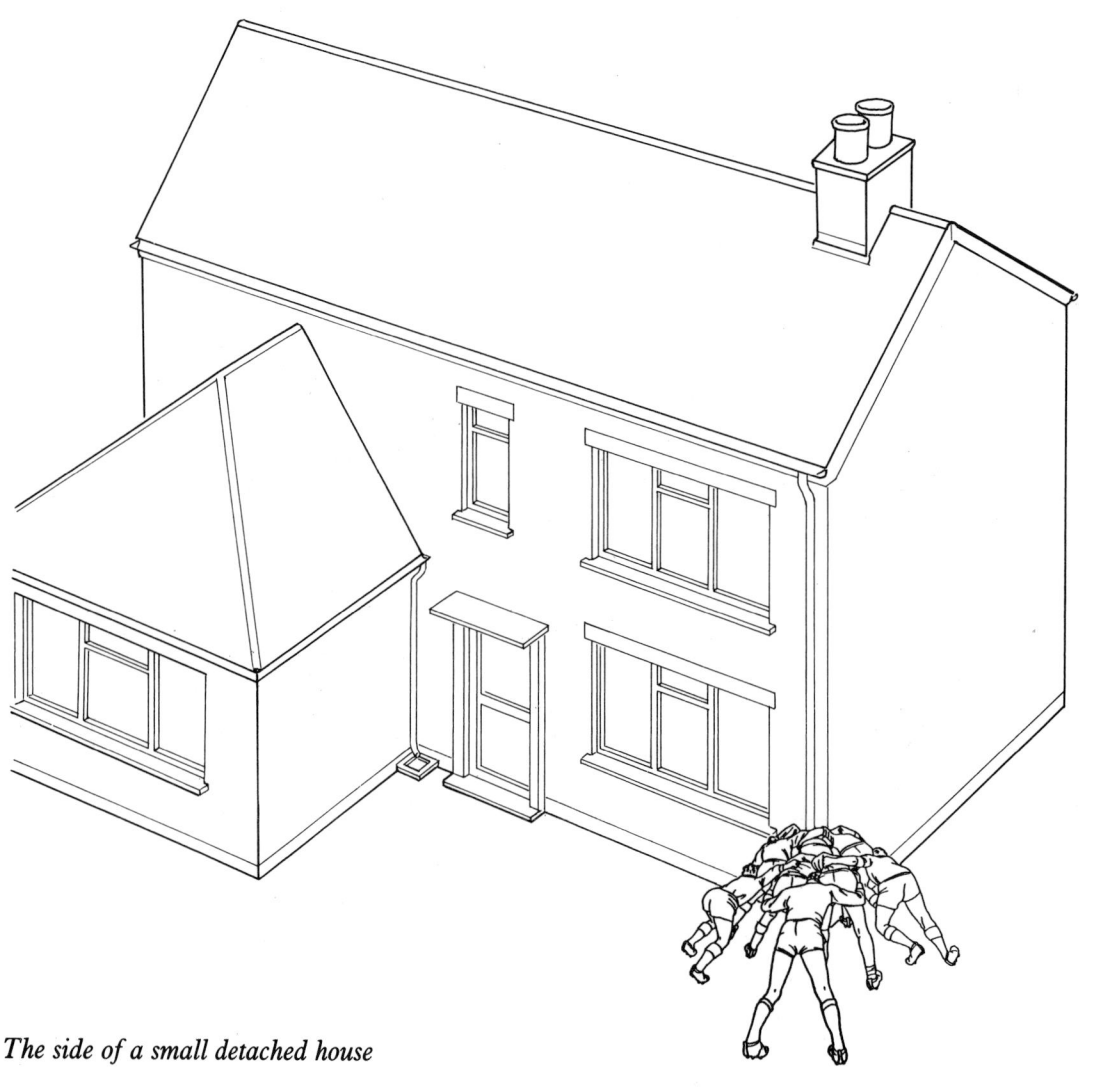

The side of a small detached house

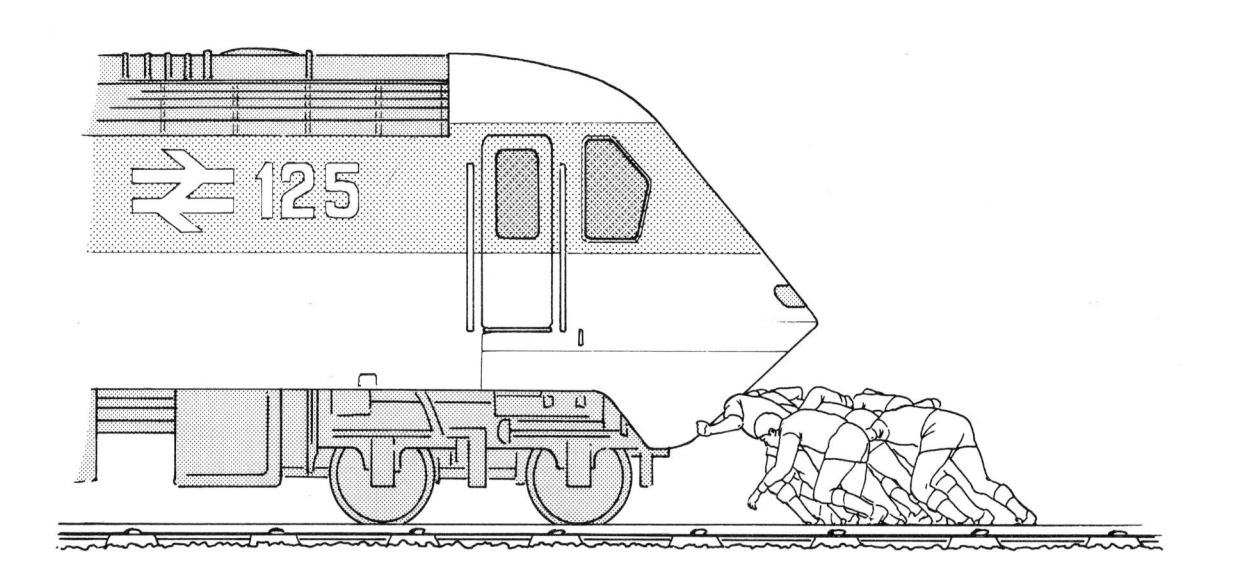

A stationary Inter City 125

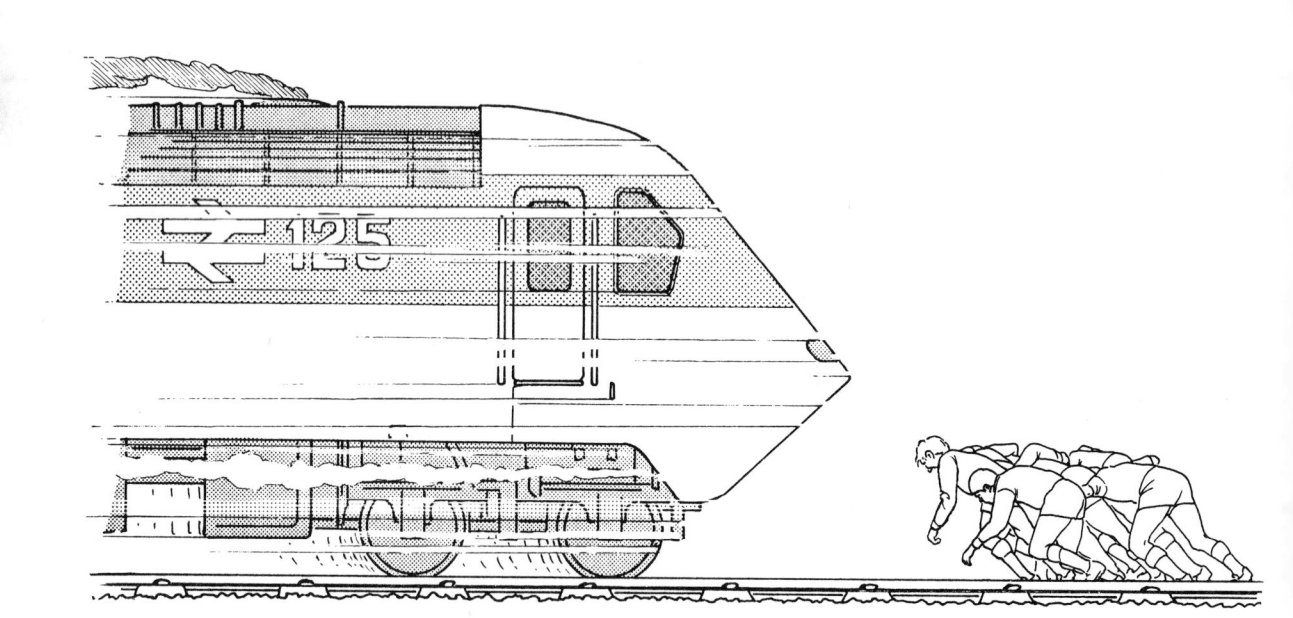

A moving Inter City 125

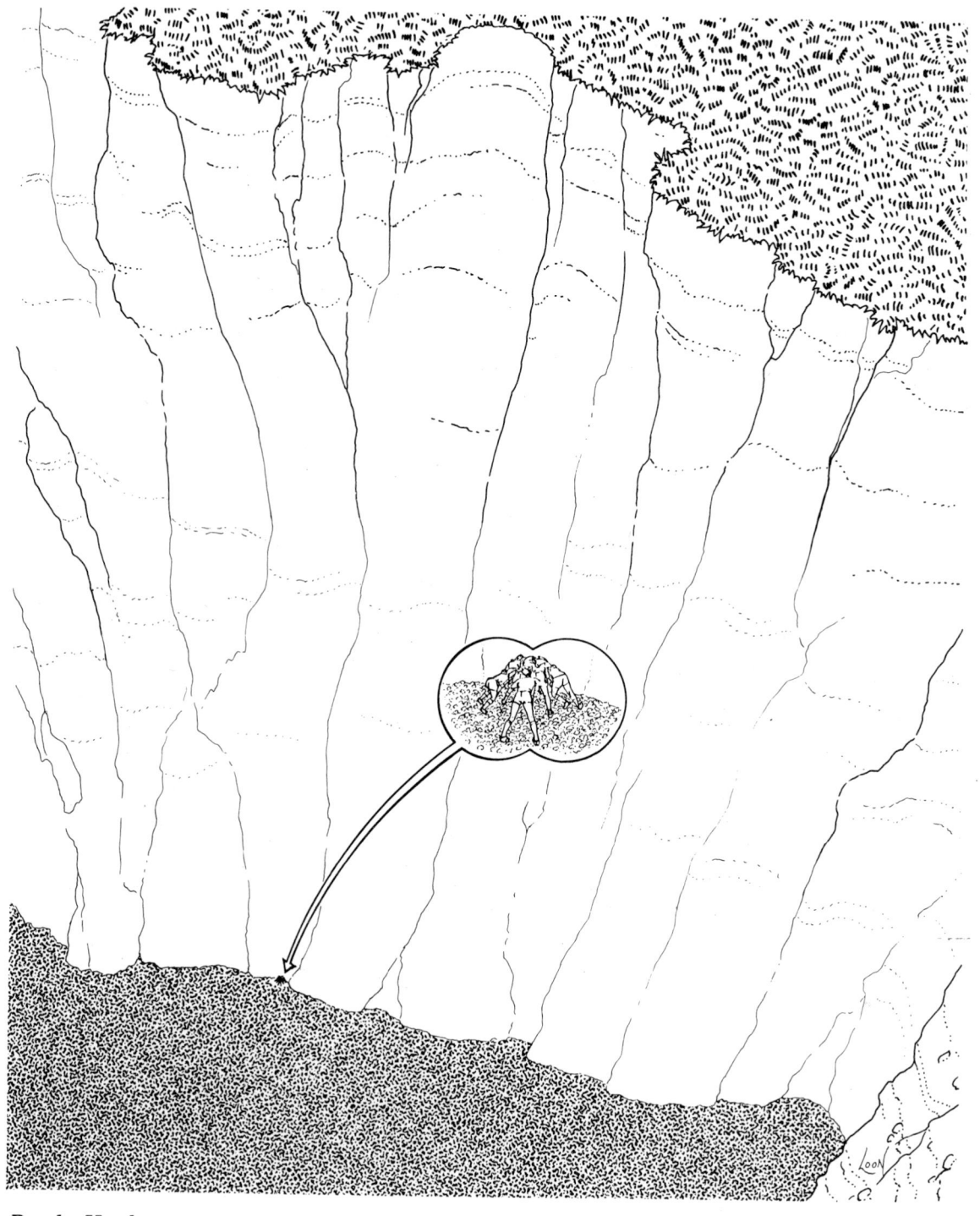

Beachy Head

The San Andreas Fault line in Southern California

The use of the corner flag

Far too many teams fail to make use of the facilities at their disposal on the pitch. This not only includes such elementary considerations as the space and the wings, but must also include more unusual facilities such as the corner flags.

Remember these are generally of sturdy construction and quite flexible. They will take the weight of a full grown man without any problem yet will spring back to shape the moment the pressure is released. This should be the source of a novel defence ploy.

Player A is caught in possession by his opponents. He has only player B with him as support. Player B should retreat to the corner flag and throw himself upon it as though it were a catapult. The effect is as though he has leant upon a coiled spring, for the pole will immediately snap back to shape throwing the player up into the air and over the heads of the menacing opponents. Player A should time his pass critically so that player B collects it in mid-flight and lands in free space with the ball a split second later.

1 MAKING A TWELVE MAN TOWER TO CUT OUT CONVERSIONS

Although there are strict rules that control the line of flight in the line out, there is little if anything about the height of any throw.

The effect is to engineer a human tower some eighteen feet high.

Teams wishing to exploit this loophole may find a simple gymnastic trick reaps rewards.

Player A sits on player B's shoulders who sits on player C's shoulders, and so forth....

The thrower need simply throw the ball in at this height to guarantee his own team wins possession.

2 HOW TO AVOID A TACKLE THE ACROBATIC WAY

This problem can be avoided by thinking ahead.

When a tackle looks unavoidable, the player in possession should slow sufficiently for two teammates to run alongside.

Practise this routine until you can clear your opponents' back line in one shot.

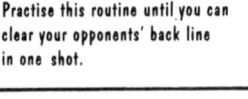

Too many teams allow promising moves to break down because they run into tackles.

They then cup their hands in front of the player in possession and just before the tackle is made they catapult player and ball into the air and over the opponent's head.

3 THE FIFTY YARD LINE-OUT THROW

Once again teams fail to make capital out of line-out through lack of ingenuity.

With practice you should be able to throw the ball fifty or more yards and reach the far touchline.

Remember that you are allowed to throw the ball as far as you like so long as it is in a straight line.

A player stationed on this touch-line ready for the throw is thus given a free catch and a chance to run at his opponents' line.

4 THE USE OF PETROLEUM JELLY

The team smears the outside of their kit with petroleum jelly before the game, making them difficult to grab hold of and bring down in a tackle.

It seems odd that a contact sport such as rugby should have failed to recognise how the contact element can be dramatically reduced by a simple trip to the chemists'.

A team covered in this way will evade even the sternest tackle, and apart from the funny looks from the chemist and an increased laundry bill, the side effects are minimal.

5 RUNNING BACKWARDS

It is surprising how many players find it difficult to avoid making a forward pass.

This is natural since our inclination is to go forward and passing backwards seems an alien intrusion.

Players finding it impossible to overcome the problem should take heart from a simple trick:

if you run backwards everywhere then all passes can now be made forwards, which is now in effect backwards, if you follow the meaning.

Teams adopting this technique tend to record slower progress upfield, plus a distinct risk of disorientation, but the number of forward passes is cut dramatically.

6 A HANDY TIP FOR SCRUM HALVES

Scrum halves invariably find themselves in the awkward position of receiving the ball from the scrum and being unsure what to do.

1.

3.
Simply return the ball straight back into the scrum.

When the ball emerges a second time from the scrum you will now have surprise on your side and it is very likely your opponents will give you a free run to goal before they realise what's what.

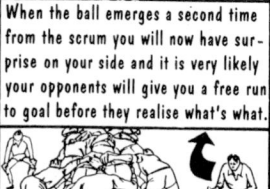

If you are caught in this way there is a simple yet rarely employed trick.

2.

4.
The effect on your opponents will be to render them totally confused and bemused.

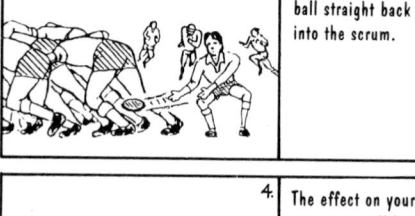

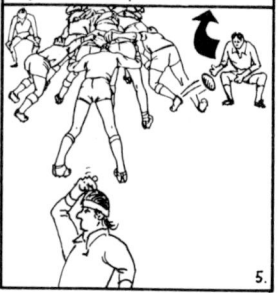

5.

Three useful moves for rugby players

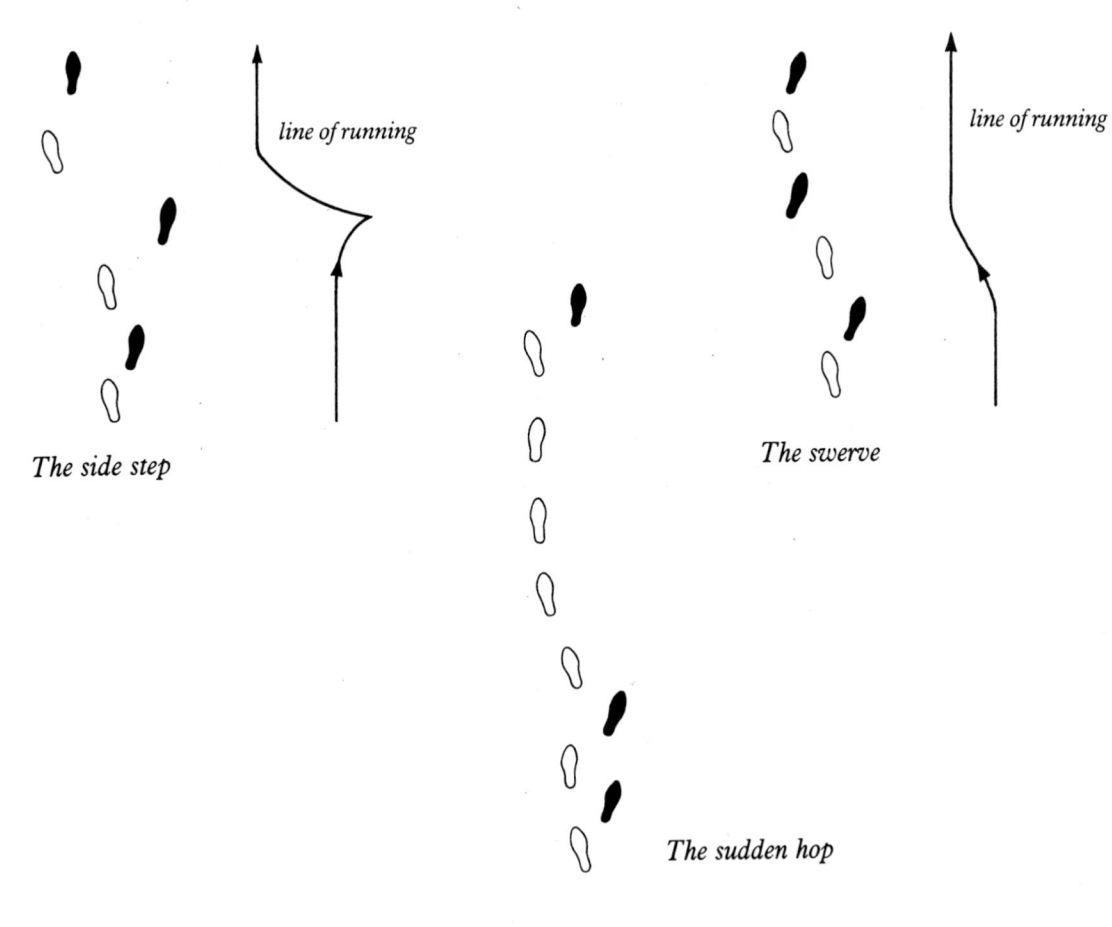

line of running

line of running

The side step

The swerve

The sudden hop

Useful things to say

Five useful things to say to a scrum half when dropping his inch-perfect pass:

- 'It's all right, I think I know what you were trying to do.'
- 'Don't worry, it's just the sort of mistake I would make.'
- 'The idea was brilliant.'
- 'Do you want me to show you what you did wrong?'
- 'I think it's great that someone's even prepared to try a pass like that.'

Five useful things to say after fumbling a simple up and under on your own twenty-five which almost certainly cost your team the match and your captain his job:

- 'Where was the support?'
- 'Technically I did everything right.'
- 'I was waiting for a call.'
- 'How d'you know I didn't mean to do that?'
- 'It was actually a very clever way of playing them offside.'

Five useful things to say after failing to make a simple conversion directly in front of the posts:

■ 'There's fourteen other people in this team, you know.'
■ 'I wanted to make a game of it.'
■ 'It's amazing how deceptive the angle is on a kick like that.'
■ 'I think you have to look wider than simply did it go between the posts.'
■ 'Look d'you want a lift home after the game or not?'

New terms

Although rugby has many terms to describe the conventional aspects of the game, it has always seemed a sad omission that there aren't sufficient terms to describe the more common bungles or mistakes. Fumble, drop catch, mishandle and knock-on are practically the only terms we have in common usage to describe a whole plethora of inept play.

I would therefore like to add my own list of *bona fide* terms for inclusion in all future rugby coaching publications.

Fribble
A simple pass is missed entirely allowing the opponents to pounce and run in for a try.

Nulp
The player kicks directly over the top of the ball sending it forward ten feet and leaving his backs cruelly exposed.

Flup
The act of tripping up for absolutely no apparent reason and landing face first in the mud.

Cloddie
A pass which travels at least twelve feet above the head of the person it was intended for.

Splod
A drop kick that goes directly up in the air and lands back down exactly where it came from.

Wurp
A drop kick which actually travels ten yards back down the pitch in the direction you've just come from.

B'dink
A diving tackle in which the tackler attempts to launch himself through the air and misses his opponent by at least ten feet.

Asplom
A move that comes to an abrupt end when the player with the ball runs head first into one of his own players.

Clud
A pass to a non-existent player.

Slable
The act of trying to catch a huge kick downfield with your eyes closed.

Noblock
The act of tripping over the ball head first.

Four training exercises for the very unfit

Sitting down is one of the easiest exercises to learn and one of the most rewarding. Practise sitting down regularly and you will be surprised how quickly you become proficient at the art. Here the author shows a perfect example of sitting down doing very little.

(Sitting down has yet to become a recognised sport by the Olympic Federation but there is hope of incorporating it into the 1996 Games.)

Kneeling down isn't quite as easy as it looks and certainly isn't as easy as sitting down, so spend plenty of time practising. Try it first with the left knee, then with the right. Then with both knees. If you find it tiring, then sit down again for a while. Here the author kneels down for nearly twenty minutes without doing anything.

Running *can be very, very tiring indeed so make sure you do lots of sitting down before and afterwards. The best way to practise running is over very short distances of two or three feet. Running on the spot is another type of running. Especially if you don't do it for very long. Another good tip is to run very slowly or not at all. In fact, standing still is very nearly the same as running, except you don't actually move, plus it isn't nearly as exhausting.*

Hurdling *is perhaps the least advisable exercise and here the author shows why. Not only do you have to run, which is quite tiring, but you have to jump over things as well, which is even more tiring. The best way to practise hurdling is in a sitting position, watching other people do it – preferably on the television. Another good idea is to run round the hurdles because in all honesty what is the point of jumping over when it's just as quick to miss it out completely. Here the author demonstrates the wrong way to hurdle which is with energy and determination.*

Here the author demonstrates the clever use of the Suzuki motorbike in clearing from defence.

Training at home and at work

Long hours at work nowadays often leave little time for training out on the park. The leisurely stroll to the practice ground after a relaxing day in the City may not now be possible and players must look at other ways of staying in trim.

This is where my home and work fitness manual comes to the fore. It is designed to allow you to train without breaking your normal regime. The main points are summarised below.

Long corridors: these give ample opportunity for speed training. Try sprinting up and down them three or four times on your way to meetings, or for extra training lay a few waste paper baskets down the middle and sprint around them. If the Chairman passes by, tell him it is part of a new time-and-motion study. Another good idea is that scourge of the training field: backwards running. Select a suitable corridor and jog down it backwards at a brisk pace. Use a briefcase as a makeshift ball. In open-plan offices it may be possible to arrange a short circuit around the workstations. Do watch out for secretaries. If they seem worried, explain it is a directive from head office.

Dining rooms: these offer the benefits of congestion and crowding, both ideal for close footwork training. Try zig-zag runs between the tables. Should you be lucky enough to work alongside fellow players, get them to act as the opposition in a game of 'tig' rugby. Your objective is to make it from one side of the room to the other without being caught. Always pay for any breakages immediately. (This game is not recommended for the executive dining room!)

Filing cabinets: a fully-loaded filing cabinet makes an excellent partner for tackling practice. Select a suitable cabinet then practise pulling it to the floor with a diving tackle. It is preferable to practise this in an empty office as the noise as it hits the ground can be considerable. Lunchtime is often a good moment. If you are caught wrestling the cabinet to the floor, explain that you had trouble with one of the drawers and were trying to find an important document. Never attempt to tackle a filing cabinet while someone is using it. Above all, never attempt to tackle a filing cabinet while someone else is trying to tackle it.

Springloaded firedoors: modern firedoors are generally counter-loaded to spring shut. It is usually possible to increase the tension of these doors. By discreet tightening you should be able to increase the tension so the door requires a full shoulder charge to open it. This makes ideal practice for fullbacks. Run at the doors at full speed and attempt to barge them open before they snap back in your face. By tightening gradually over a period you should be able to increase the tension without attracting attention. If staff find themselves trapped in the office and unable to get out, admit to nothing and feign abject concern.

At home: try and look for simple things that you can do amongst your everyday chores. Jump over the coffee table when you walk through the living room. Lift the fridge up and down three times before getting the milk out. Before going to bed, run up and down the stairs ten times (warn the neighbours, especially if stairs are communal) and construct a simple circuit training set-up with an ironing board, a garden roller and a Black and Decker Workmate (details on request).

4

INJURIES

First aid for rugby players

I reprint below, in full, the official guide to first aid on the rugby field.

In the event of an injury on the field follow the course of action described below:

1 Take the wet sponge.
2 Administer it to the injured area.
3 If pain persists dampen sponge and try again.

Injuries

As a rugby player you are likely to sustain a number of injuries. They are unlikely to prove fatal, and even if they are you should still be able to carry on playing. The correct name given by doctors for an injury sustained during a rugby match is termed 'rugger mortis' since the act is very similar to rigor mortis, only a lot stiffer.

A good tip is to arm yourself with a list of the more common ailments. This won't prevent injury but will lessen the shock when you come round in the casualty ward unable to move or speak. Carry the list round with you together with a note to ask the medical staff to tick those which you have contracted.

Those injuries common among rugby players are:

broken leg
broken arm
dislocated hip
dislocated shoulder
dislocated ankle
dislocated head
cracked teeth
broken nose
fractured skull
severe bruising
bruised ribs
broken ribs
spare ribs (rare)
barbecued spare ribs (very rare)
concussion
death
acute death
broken jaw
broken everything
broken marriage
broken wind (in the plunge afterwards)
stab wounds
all the above

By contrast there are a number of complaints that the average rugby player is unlikely to fall victim to. It is a small crumb of comfort as you lie there, a mutilated punch bag, immobile, every bone in your body broken and crying out for sympathy, but it could be worse. Just think of the following afflictions you almost certainly won't be suffering from and you will at once feel better.

Those injuries which you are not likely to suffer from include:

Housemaid's knee
Housemaid's shin
Housemaid's scrotum
Swamp fever
Mustard gas poisoning
Pre-menstrual tension
Bubonic plague
Foot and mouth disease
Myxomatosis
Senile dementia
Jogger's nipple   (only caught through intimate or sexual contact with another jogger)
Logger's nipple   (only caught through intimate or sexual contact with another logger or lumberjack)
Pregnancy   (can occasionally be caught in loose rucks in mixed rugby games, or if you share a towel with a female player)
Nappy rash
Wilkinson's disease   (unless you happen to be called Wilkinson)
Woodworm

Accident report form

This form has been specially prepared to facilitate quick attention in hospital casualty departments. It should be handed to the doctor immediately upon arrival.

Nature of injury ....

How did it happen? ....

When did it happen? ....

What caused the accident: boot/knee/elbow/head/finger/ starting handle/brick/crowbar/trouser zip/other [please delete as appropriate]

Checklist of organs and limbs upon entering hospital (please give a brief list of the approximate number and position of all organs and limbs for reference purposes) [enclose sketch where necessary]
....

....

Can you describe how the injury occurred? ....
    (if no, say 'no')

State position at time ....
    (e.g. prop forward, hooker, fullback, referee, spectator, passenger on passing bus etc.)

What is the most junior rank of medical staff you will allow to treat you?
    Consultant
    Senior Registrar
    Junior Registrar
    Staff nurse
    Student nurse
    Hospital porter
    Hospital cat
[tick as appropriate]

1

Would you like us to arrange a quote for double glazing while you are in hospital?   YES/NO

Do you know the third verse to Eskimo Nell?   YES/NO
(If yes, please enclose on separate sheet.)

Who is your favourite female singer? ....

Have you ever suffered from any of the following illnesses before: death? acute death? chronic death? If the operation you require isn't possible is there any other operation you would accept instead?
(if so, state below)

....

Next-of-kin ....

Next-of-kin's next-of-kin ....

Next-of-kin's next-of-kin's next-of-kin ....

....

(Actually we don't really need to know all of these but it does take a long time for the doctor to see you in casualty and going through your family tree might help to pass the time.)

Sign and date ....

[WARNING: Do keep a duplicate and attach it to the patient. In busy hospitals there is a danger that the form may be assumed to refer to the wrong patient and a simple broken leg treated with complex neurosurgery.]

2

Parts of the body to bandage

One of the most important aspects of the game of rugby is the art of bandaging. Few sports demand the anatomy be swaddled in quite the way that rugby does. Indeed there is debate whether Tutankhamen might not have been given a county trial purely on the basis of his bandages.

Bandages show that you mean business and have the crippling injuries to prove it. They also show that you probably don't like showering and have hit on a novel way of protecting yourself from getting muddy.

To achieve even moderate success on the rugby field you will therefore need to become proficient in the ancient art of bandaging. However, it is wise not to let enthusiasm run away with common sense and it is worth remembering that only certain limbs and organs are suitable for wrapping.

Right things to bandage:
wrist
knee (left)
knee (right)
scalp
ankle
thigh

Wrong things to bandage:
neck
nose
nipples
willy
someone else's willy (especially if you haven't asked permission first)

sports' bag
half-time lemons
bottle of Matey bath oil
car

Remember that elaborate bandaging can take time. Do allow yourself an extra half-hour or so in the changing room before the game if you are planning to bandage major parts of the body. Remember, a big bandaging job can take a long time especially as you yourself become progressively more bound up with more and more bandaging. Hurried bandaging is often worse than no bandaging at all. There is nothing worse than rushing the job and ending up with both legs wrapped tightly together. Nor is it acceptable eventually to make it on to the pitch ten minutes before the final whistle armed with the feeble excuse that you have spent the last two hours in the changing hut bandaging yourself up.

Suitable fabrics for bandages:
crêpe

Unsuitable fabrics for bandages:
old carpet tiles
old socks
old panties
sticky backed plastic
Laura Ashley remnants
The Mappa Mundi
that old J-cloth you usually use to clean out the cat's litter tray
A greasy oven glove that slipped down the back of the cooker two years ago

Right: The author going through his elaborate twenty-seven point conversion ritual. (The kick was missed.)

5

RITUALS

Conversion rituals

If five percent of the effort that goes into the superstitions surrounding spot kicking went into the actual act of kicking the ball itself, then it is fairly safe to say that most fullbacks would double their points' tally overnight. Should the laces be placed to the left or to the right? Should the ball be tipped slightly forward or slightly back? Should the kicker take ten steps or twelve? And should he approach from the left or the right?

The ritual doesn't confine itself to the game. Endless hours are spent out on the pitch in solitary practice before the game, practising and re-practising. Three from the left. Three from the right. Then three from dead centre. And if any kick misses, the whole ritual is broken and may have to be repeated again but in a different order, or in the same order but with a change of approach. Or . . . well, you can see the permutations are

endless. If the captain didn't come and forcibly drag the hapless kicker off the pitch it is fair to say he would still be practising before, during, and even after the actual game itself has finished.

My own personal remedy to the folklore surrounding spot kicking is quite simple. Always place the laces three-eighths of an inch to the left of centre, very slightly off centre, the ball four degrees from the vertical in favour of whichever side the posts are on, while the kicker should approach at 32 degrees off centre, taking thirteen and a half steps precisely, except where the kick is less than eight feet from a line drawn perpendicularly to both posts, joined by an arc with the radius of twice the square root of the width of the pitch.

The actual mechanics of this calculation are in fact totally irrelevant as to whether the kick fails or succeeds, but the time and effort spent working it out quite take the mind off the kick at hand and reduce the risk of a panicky attempt.

While a certain amount of ritual is to be accepted with spot kicks, it is wise to draw the line at some point. The following are *not* permitted:

- Ritualistic slaughter of a virgin goat in praise of the Lord High God of spot kickers.
- Pagan prayers, scribed in a tabernacle circle with thirty other pagan worshippers.
- Drinking the fresh blood of a fellow player to give you strength to make the kick.
- Spiritualistic pre-match bathing of the ball in a bath of oxen urine, followed by the release of six white doves immediately prior to the kick.
- Presentation of a pair of sheep's testicles to the line judge in the hope that your wish of a good kick will be granted.
- Wild, frenetic snogging of the ball as a token of good luck (although a pert little kiss on top of the ball is sometimes allowed for very important kicks).

Voodoo rugby

A new, and potentially lethal, form of crowd abuse comes from the Caribbean where the ancient art of voodoo has been adapted to the modern art of tackling. The system is quite simple, a voodoo effigy of an opponent is made in wax and at the critical moment that a tackle is about to be brought a pin is stuck in the opponent's arm or leg, or wherever, causing him to pull up in pain. The pin is then removed, the pain disappears, and the hapless player left to grasp at thin air.

That is the principle. Unfortunately, early trials have proved less than successful for a number of reasons.

Firstly, it is remarkably difficult to make an authentic effigy of most players. Once the gum shield and headband are on and a liberal coating of fresh mud applied then one player tends to look much like the rest. In one test case, the pin was inserted and a player on the opposite side of the field, fully fifty yards away from the action, pulled up in agony. In a second case, the player with the ball suffered the same fate and lay writhing in pain without even reaching the tackle. In a third case, a lady walking her dog round the perimeter of the pitch suddenly keeled over in distress. Clearly if the system is to work a great deal of work must be done to remove this confusion.

Secondly, even where the correct player is maimed the effect may not be altogether as hoped for. Since co-ordination between mind and action in the lower leagues is often rudimentary, any act which interferes with this balance may in fact turn out to be productive rather than counter-productive. In one case a player who was, at best, hopeless in the tackle, proved to be far more effective with a paralysed limb. In another case a player who constantly misjudged his assaults by several yards found that with one leg immobile and out of use he would lurch unerringly into the path of an approaching player and make a quite reasonable tackle. Equally, at the top end of the game, pain is not something that readily troubles the average player. A man used to having bites taken out of him and his face sat on by a sixteen-stone Welsh forward is hardly likely to take notice of a sharp or sudden pain to his arm or leg. He will naturally assume he has been bitten/hit/kicked/knived and will think no more of it.

The third and final problem arises from the respect accorded the art of voodoo and its ability to trade fear and trepidation in its followers. In traditional societies, steeped in the mystique of the voodoo High Priest, this carries ultimate authority. No-one challenges the voodoo maker. On the rugby field the effect is somewhat different. A player, on finding the reason for his incapacity, is just as likely to hobble over to the side of the pitch and punch the voodoo spell worker on the nose as he is to bow down in sufferance. Indeed, while the player might suffer a sharp pain in the leg or arm, the voodoo spellcaster might very well end up with his entire body in plaster and his legs broken in eight places.

Showers

A great deal of the appeal of rugby is in the camaraderie, and nowhere is that camaraderie more apparent than in the post-match changing rooms. The game is steeped in post-match rituals and none more so than the shower-and-tub. The code of behaviour is strict and unwavering. While lewd and boisterous singing is allowed, light operetta, close harmony work, minstrel singing, gregorian chants and all forms of romantic ballads are forbidden. Equally forbidden are a number of items which one might otherwise be tempted to take into the shower room.

Principal items that rugby players are not allowed to take into the showers or tub:

- decorative Disney soaps
- scented bath salts
- bath toys, toy boats, plastic ducks or clockwork Henry Hippos
- frilly towels or towels with fancy embroidery work
- Matey shower gel
- your mother
- shower cap
- hand flannel in the form of a glove puppet
- Crabtree and Evelyn Flowers of Passion bubble bath
- your camera
- a powder puff and talcum powder
- cuticle scissors and nail file
- Keith Chegwin
- Dagenham Girl Pipers

6

THE ADVANCED COACHING MANUAL

The rugby coaching manual

At this point in the book I had hoped to bring you my personal photo-coaching manual based on years of experience in the game. Unfortunately, at the last moment a fellow player who had arranged to stand in with me on the pictures, and who shall remain nameless, though he is in fact called Tony Brooks, found he was unavailable and cried off. I therefore was left with no alternative but to enlist my mum and family to help out. While this naturally detracts slightly from the value of some photographs, I hope that they still provide a valuable insight. Indeed, for those players who happen to play against my mum their value may in fact be enhanced.

HAND OFF

Tuck the ball firmly into the chest

Use your free hand to fend off the opponent's tackle

Handing off against the head can throw
your opponent off balance

Allow your speed and
momentum to carry you
through

DIRECT RUNNING

Sometimes it is possible to open a route to goal by running directly at your opponents

Where opponents block your way run directly at them

Use your head and shoulders to counter their tackle

And allow your body weight to
push them aside

Direct running like this can break through an
opponent's defence and open a direct run to
goal

TACKLING

Left: Always approach as low down as possible when tackling

TIMING THE TACKLE

Below: Try and time your tackle to catch the opponent off guard (in this case Mum was feeling a bit tired so she sat down to rest her legs but hopefully you still get the general idea)

RUCKING

This is a situation that many players find themselves in

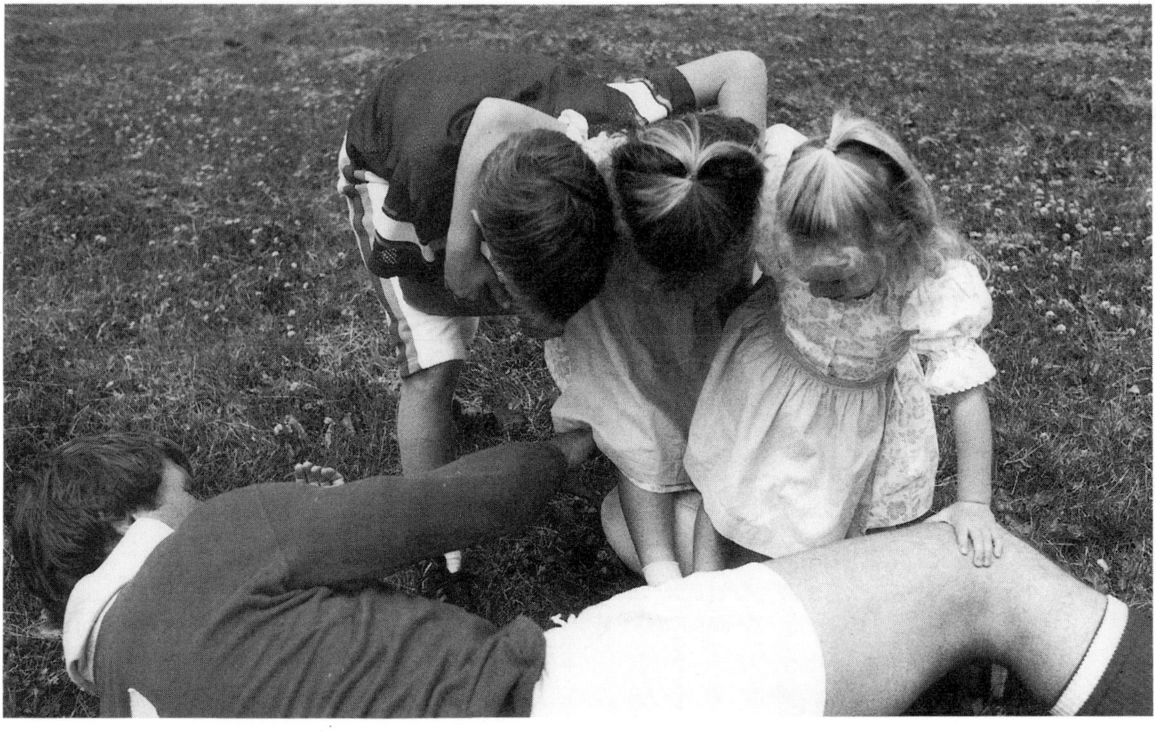

Use your body to protect the ball and prevent your opponents gaining possession

KICKING

Note the correct line of
body and toe

The body must be over the
ball at the time of impact

Extra loft may be achieved
by leaning back and
allowing the foot to travel
through the ball

By following these simple
rules a successful kick can
be made every time

THE BALL'S EYE VIEW

Most rugby books confine themselves simply to the players' perspective, while ignoring the very important role played by the ball itself. Below is a special coaching supplement designed especially for the ball and giving a unique ball's eye perspective on the game, taken by a hidden camera actually inside a rugby ball.

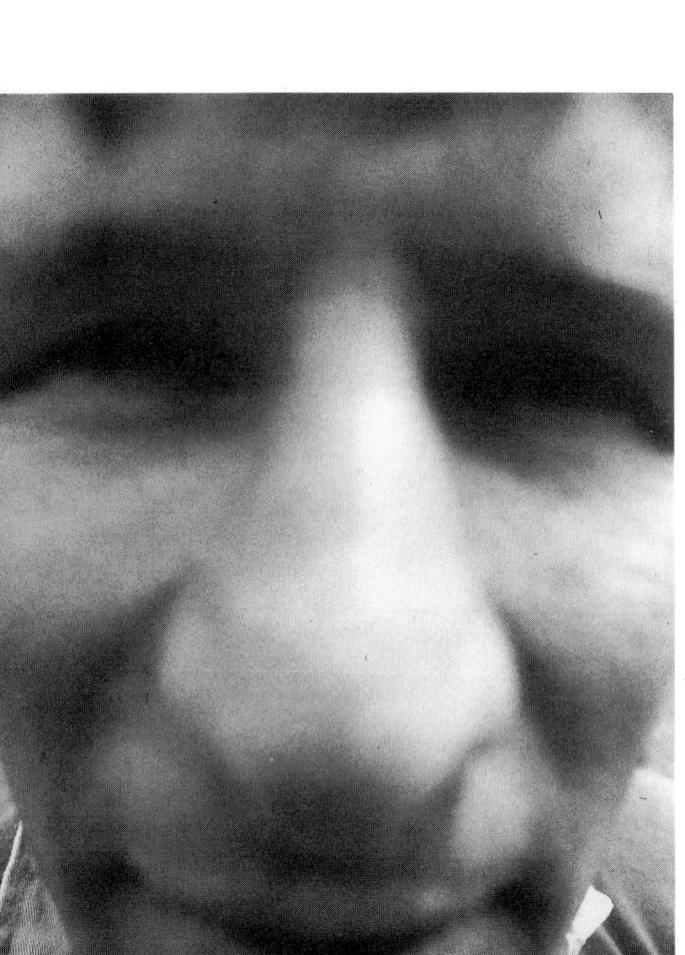

The ball's eye view of an up and under (going up)

The ball's eye view of a knock-on against the head

The ball's eye view of an up and under (going down)

The ball's eye view of being
kicked

The ball's eye view of being
trodden on

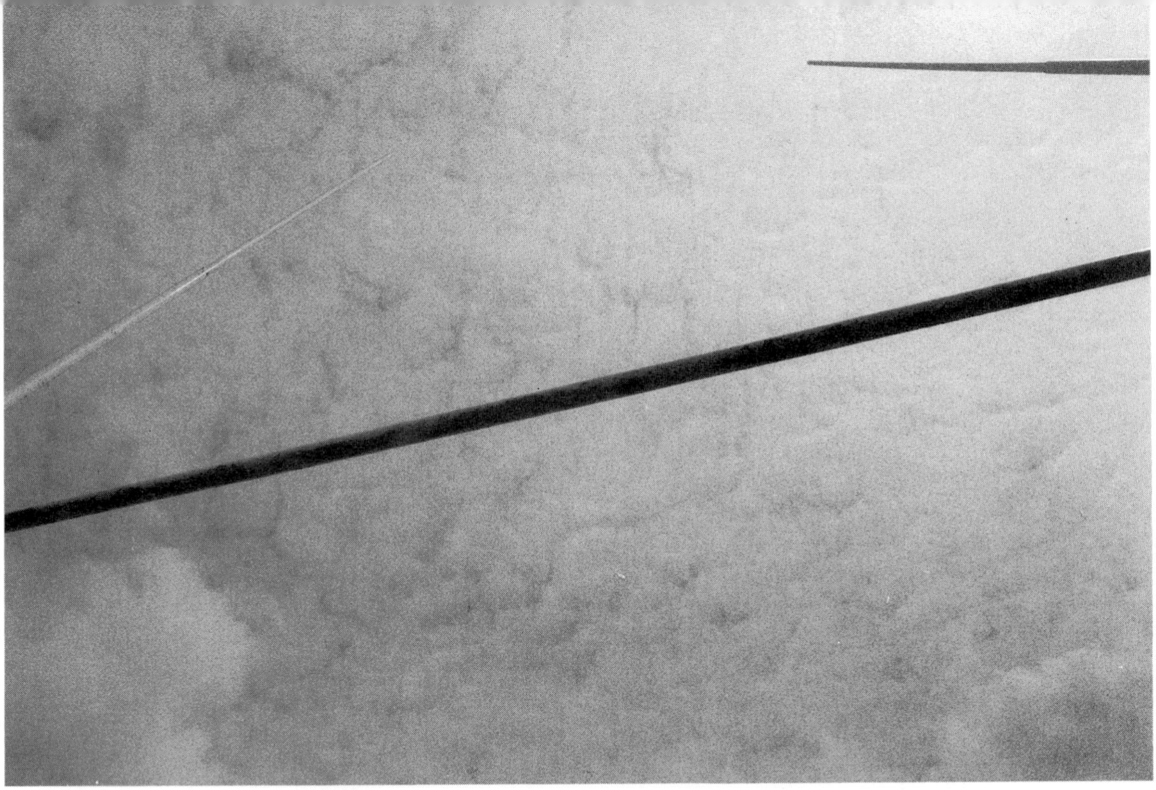

Above: The ball's eye view of a successful conversion

Left: The ball's eye view of coming out from a scrum

7
THE ART OF RUGBY

The rugby gallery

1 *Stained glass; Christ's Devotion to Rugby (South Transept Window, Rheims Cathedral)*

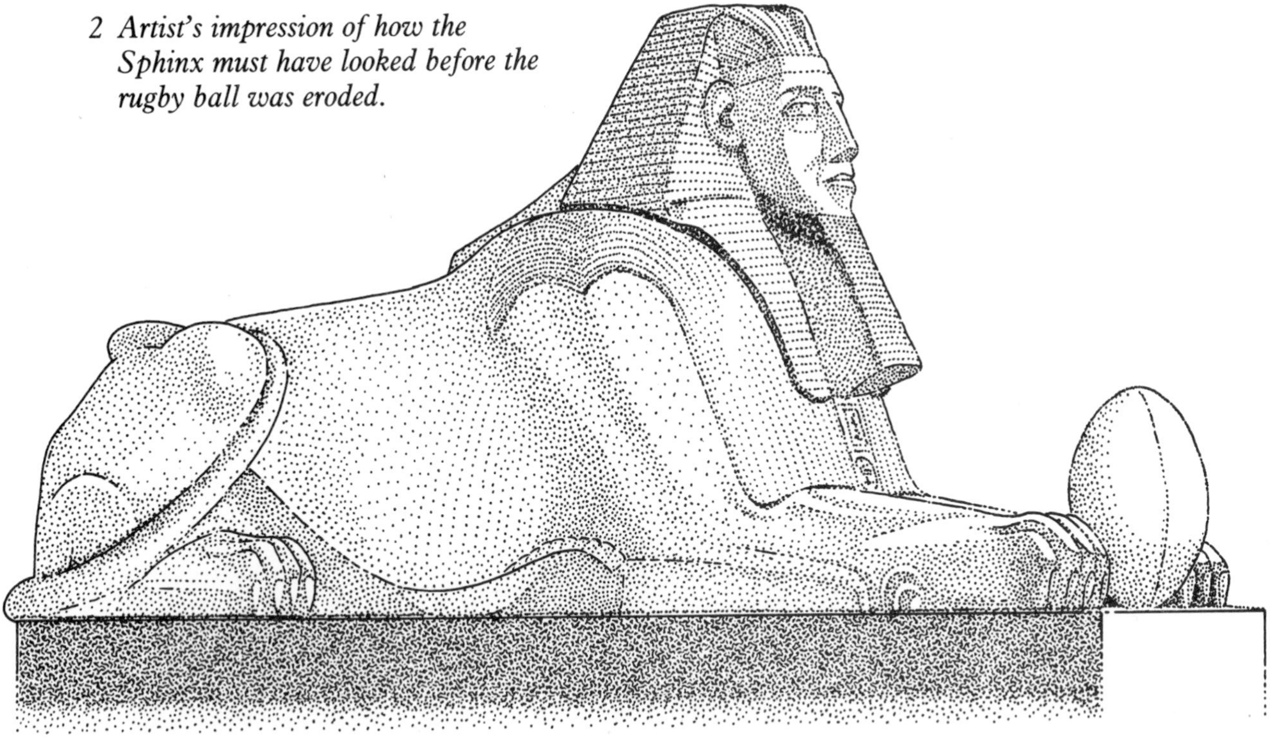

2 Artist's impression of how the Sphinx must have looked before the rugby ball was eroded.

3 Hieroglyphics. The inscription reads: 'A clever reverse pass splits open the Genoan defence and leaves the flanker free to run in from twenty yards.'

4 *Indian girl (in rugby kit)*

The David Bailey jock strap collection

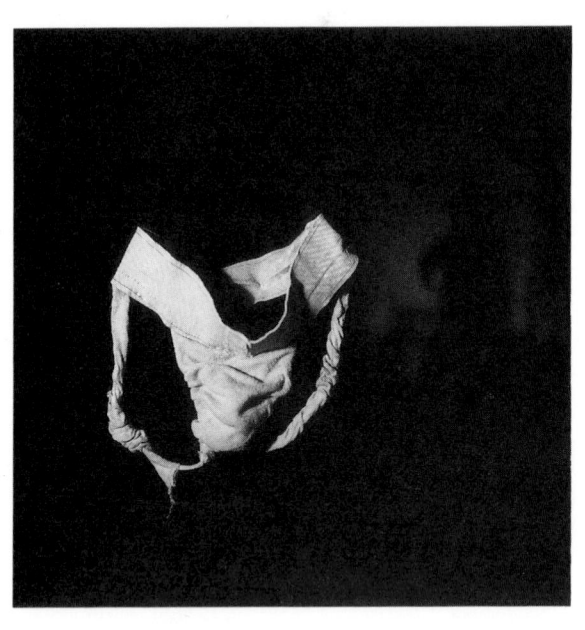

Le Strap du Jock
(private collection)

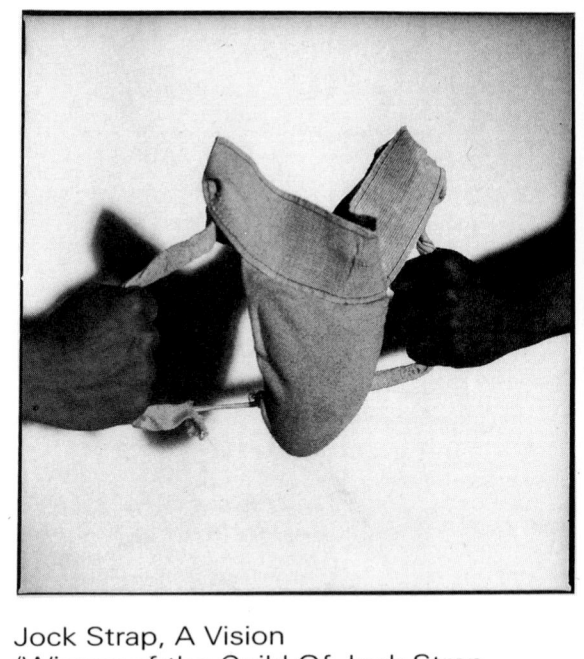

Jock Strap, A Vision
(Winner of the Guild Of Jock Strap
Photographers award, 1976)

The jock strap as art

Few players realise that the jock strap has
been the influence for many contemporary
photographic exhibitions. This particular
collection was first shown in 1984 and is one of
the finest.

A Jock Strap
(after Man Ray)

Forgotten Yesterdays, A Study In Jock
Straps
(from the Post Modernist Jockstrap
exhibition at the Hayward Gallery)

Jock Strap & Scrum Cap
(still life)

8

ORGANISATION OF THE GAME

Regionalism

While national pride may shine like an ember in every supporter's eye, it is nothing compared to the rivalry that takes place within nations.

The Scottish lines are drawn more firmly than Culloden with the Edinburgh teams of Watsonians and the like drawn in direct bloodlust opposition to the Border teams of Kelso, Hawick and Melrose. Apart from the two camps wishing to lay one another to the sword in a bloodbath of carnage and dismemberment, they both show scant regard for the teams of Glasgow who waste little time in reciprocating the feeling.

Similarly in Ireland, while the sport transcends the border and unites the island, there is a well-marked division between the players who have come through the Catholic fee-paying schools and the Protestant state schools. Wales alone does not seem to have such civil strife, but it re-ignites again in France where the Paris-based teams are pitted against their countrymen in the South West. Finally, in England the division lies between the public school image as supported by well-starched tie of Twickenham, and the ordinary clodhopper as supported by the grass roots of the game.

The outcome of this insane regional rivalry is to distort any backing to the point that a team may find itself the beneficiaries of bizarre support. I have played for English teams in the Hawick Sevens who have been drawn against an Edinburgh-based team and enjoyed the vocal support of the local populace. In the next round we have found our opponents to be from the Borders themselves and our support now came from the Edinburgh contingent who bayed against us in the previous round. Finally, we have been drawn in the next round against a Glasgow team and the Edinburgh and Borders fans have joined together to back us. Goodness knows what would have happened had we been drawn against a French team; I imagine most non-partisan fans would be so confused they would hedge their bets and shout for both teams. It is all very confusing.

And the matter becomes even more complex when the Lions' squad is picked. Here is the opportunity for the different nations to mingle and merge as one, drawn together by the flag of international friendship. But the early days are a minefield of diplomacy. Players who don't even speak the same tongue will gel together far quicker than players who might share the same national shirt but be poles apart regionally. And the skill in the early days is not in forging an international bond but in preventing civil bitterness erupting into outright warfare.

In time, and faced with a common foe (viz Australia or the All Blacks), the lines (and the Lions) do unite and very quickly rivalries are forgotten. Well, at least until the next league season when everyone welcomes the chance to open up old scores and bite chunks out of the fellow countryman they slapped on the back in friendship as they bade farewell at the end of the Lions' tour.

Career structure

For the aspiring rugby novice I list below the natural career structure for the go-ahead player:

Captain fifth fifteen
Captain fourth fifteen
Captain third fifteen
Captain second fifteen
Deputy Captain first fifteen
Captain first fifteen
Captain drinking team
President drinking team
Life President drinking team

National leagues

The advent of the National League system has brought to rugby a phenomena never before known, namely naked competitiveness.

Previously teams were naturally keen to win and would exhibit all the rabid signs, but it was unfocused, undirected, the simple enthusiasm of they-beat-us-last-time-so-we'll-knock-the-stuffing-out-of-them-this-time-around. In other words: amateur enthusiasm.

The National League set-up has changed all that. Now teams play for league status. The result has been to alter radically the way the game is perceived.

Nowadays a team may play the same opponents three times in a season, twice in non-competitive games and once in the league. The league game is the only encounter that matters. Results in the other two encounters bear no resemblance to the outcome of the league challenge. Indeed they are very often in inverse relation to league form, for captains mindful of the next league fixture are apt to pull out any first team players for fear of losing them to injury. And the better the squad, the more likely the list of withdrawals is to grow.

Thus a long respected friendly between two sides may end up slogged out by a selection of oddments and renegades from the fifth and sixth fifteens, and have not the slightest resemblance to the corresponding league fixture.

Is this a bad thing? It is hard to say. It means players who would not have stood an earthly of playing for the first fifteen now get a regular chance to pull on the prestigious top flight shirt, and it means that comparatively minor outfits may score remarkable and unexpected wins against outfits from the top division.

The difference between League and Union

Over the years a considerable amount has been written about the division in the game. My purpose here in this briefest of accounts is to distil the argument to its bare essentials and to identify the major contrasts.

In order of descending importance, the differences are:

1 Rugby League is televised on a Saturday and Rugby Union on a Sunday.

2 Rugby Union players like to support the Olympian ideal, whereas Rugby League players like to support a wife and two kids.

3 Rugby League players pay tax, Rugby Union players get expenses.

4 In Rugby League absolutely no-one at all has their own teeth.

5 In Rugby League a top team might attract 30,000 fans a match, whereas in Rugby Union a top team might attract 30,000 a season.

6 In Rugby Union hitting another player is considered a terrible offence, whereas in Rugby League it is considered honest gritty enthusiasm.

7 Rugby League players get muddier than Rugby Union players.

8 Rugby League and Rugby Union are two different sports with absolutely nothing at all in common with each other except for the shape of the ball.

9

THE SOCIAL SIDE

After the game

The post-match rituals are often more important than the game itself. Of course with the modern game and the more professional perspective the traditional booze-up into the small hours has given way to a quick orange juice and an early night in many club houses.

But where the Post-Match Tradition (or PMT) is still honoured, the custom has changed little and like *The Beano* survives by its resistance to change.

To list the variety of games and rules would require more space than this book can allot. But basically they can be summarised in this one encompassing law:

'The sole aim of all games is to consume as much alcohol as possible and to make this possible all games should consist of a series of rules that become totally incomprehensible after two pints, and totally irrelevant after five. Any failure to observe the rules should be penalised by a fine, the fine being a requirement to drink yet more alcohol. If in any doubt whether a penalty has been incurred a drink should be consumed just to be on the safe side. Players blatantly breaking the rules simply to get a free drink should be penalised by having to consume a second drink as well.'

By observing this one principle it should be possible for anyone to design their own post-match game. Try to include as many of the following as possible:

1 Physical discomfort
All games should involve a considerable amount of physical discomfort and ridicule. A combination of two or preferably all of: standing on one's head, in a bucket, with a pickled onion between one's teeth, with one leg behind one's back, etc etc is a good starting-off point.

2 Spillage
Spillage is a very important element of post-match games. These games should involve beer mugs being balanced on heads or on mountains of other beer mugs or on any other unstable object. Any spilt beer should be mopped up with beer mats which should then become part of the game.

3 Singing
Most games involve singing. The song should be obscure and involve pointing at various parts of the body. It should be bawdy and have a chorus that even the most comatose of drunks can follow.

4 Food

Food sometimes plays a part in the game. It is a good idea if the food is available to be used as a weapon and has to be thrown or tossed about throughout the evening. A buffet supper can help. Try and select food that is messy or difficult to handle and which can't be removed from hair or clothing. The food can be used as an extra penalty in the game to be consumed in addition to the drink.

5 Rudery

It is a good idea if the game affords some opportunity for the players to remove their trousers and moon. Alternatively incorporate a new 'mooning' law during the evening. Do not explain how the law works but at regular intervals call for all the players to drop their pants.

6 Danger

Finally it is useful if the game carries some aspect of danger. Even if it is only explaining to your wife what happened when you arrive home drunk at three in the morning with no trousers, several slices of pizza bread smeared all down your shirt front and an individual fruit pie in your top pocket.

The Welsh file

In general a rugby player need only prove himself on the pitch to get a game with his local team. But in Wales there is much more to it. You have to prove your Welshness before selection. The following are the main elements you should concentrate on:

Drinking

Very important. You will need to drink at least eighteen pints a day. Double this on match days (more if you are actually playing). Practise regularly. Get a friend to help. Get a friend to help your friend. Get a friend to help your friend helping your friend.

Singing

Also very important. You won't fit into a Welsh team if you can't sing. Take lessons. If desperate, employ a trained person to throw their voice for you. He can stand in the corner and cover for you on song nights.

Pride and passion

Every Welshman burns with pride and passion for his nation. In England this is called nationalism or jingoism or 'a typical Tunbridge Wells voter' and is a bad thing. But in Wales this is a good thing. You will find this awkward at first. Start by listening to Welsh poetry for three or four hours a night preferably while standing in wet wellingtons. This should give you the browbeaten, withered look of the arch Welshman. Or sit with a bottle of pickled onions underneath your nose while watching the Welsh International on television to 'train' your eyes to mist over and fill with tears.

A quick way to bone up on your Welsh is with my rapid revision sheet. This allows you to become proficient in Welshness in about two minutes flat and is a good way to convince any Welsh club selection committee of your credibility plus it is useful when playing the Welsh version of Trivial Pursuits.

The Welsh revision sheet

Famous Welsh recording artistes:
Shakin' Stevens
Bonnie Tyler
Max Boyce

Famous Welsh TV stars:
Harry Secombe
Ryan & Ronnie
That woman from Hi de Hi
Max Boyce

Principal Welsh exports:
coal
sheep
Max Boyce

Famous Welsh Football Teams:
Cardiff
Swansea City
Wrexham
Newport County

World Cups that Wales have starred in:

Famous Welsh artists:
the man who drew the Super Ted TV series

National animal:
the sheep

Famous Welsh sports:
sheepdog trials
sheep worrying
sheep dipping
anything else at all to do with sheep

Spoken Welsh:
Welsh is a very easy language to learn. Simply put an 'LL' before the start of every word and add six extra 'y's to every sentence.

Welsh national costume:
Wellingtons and a raincoat

Famous Welsh inventions:
the coracle
the holiday cottage
the bobble hat

Places to visit if staying in Wales:
England

If diagnosed Welsh positive

The correct term for being diagnosed Welsh is 'Welsh positive'. There is no known cure. Early symptoms include a sudden interest in leeks and a fatal liking for Max Boyce.

The Englishman in Wales

English players joining Welsh rugby clubs invariably suffer from 'chronicus taffyitis' or 'acute Welshness' or 'a real pain in the arse' which is a serious illness that causes them to become fanatically Welsh. Those suffering from 'chronicus taffyitis' or 'St David's dance' overcompensate drastically for their English upbringing and become more Welsh than the Welsh themselves (if this is possible). Watch out for enrolment at night school to learn Welsh and any sudden or unnatural attraction to sheep.

By contrast Welsh players joining English clubs do not swing the opposite way and acquire English habits. Quite the reverse in fact. A Welshman selected for a Home

Counties side is likely to re-discover his Welsh heritage with a vengeance and will take upon himself the stand of a one-man crusade.

Thus, in ascending order of Welshness:

1 The English – NOT VERY WELSH

2 The Welsh – VERY WELSH
3 The Englishman at Welsh rugby club – VERY VERY WELSH
4 The Welshman at an English rugby club VERY VERY VERY VERY WELSHY INDEED

Welsh players

Welsh forwards are either:
a) Small and physical
b) Fat and physical
c) Thin and physical
or
d) Physical and physical

Welsh backs are either:
a) Slight dark and nifty
b) Nifty dark and slight

or
c) Dark slight and nifty

Number 10: There is a story that says you could ask any man in Wales to play Number 10 and they wouldn't let you down. This is a myth. I happen to know there is at least one man in Rhyl who would be absolutely hopeless.

Line calls

By employing their own language in line and scrum calls, the Welsh have enjoyed a small but useful advantage over their opponents. It is possible for English teams playing in Wales to counter this by prudent selection. You will need in your side a Welsh translator to translate the call into English; a code expert to crack the code and discover what it says; two further experts to help with the deciphering and check the solution; a stenographer to provide rapid copy and to take down a written copy of the final version; clerical back up to support the team and ensure all paperwork is kept up to date; a training officer to supervise all the training on the clerical side and to ensure a structural training programme is maintained; a radio operator to call up assistance

should it be required; and a tea boy to provide tea and refreshments as necessary.

In short, any fifteen hoping to crack the Welsh line call code should comprise:

1 Translator
1 Code Expert
2 Assistant Code Experts
·1 Stenographer
3 Clerical Assistants
2 Junior Clerical Assistants
2 Files clerks
1 Training Officer
1 Radio Operator
1 Tea boy

Equipped in this way the team should be able to crack virtually every call in twenty seconds (which is fifteen seconds after the ball has been delivered but good enough to claim a definite psychological victory). Obviously, on the negative side, a team selected in this way is likely to be hopeless at rugby and suffer a humiliating defeat.

Footnote

The other important thing that should be noted about the Welsh is that they are without doubt the world's greatest rugby nation and that the abuse launched above has been brought about by a crushing inferiority complex that vents itself in wild and slanderous jealousy and is in no way meant as an attack on the Welsh who are wonderful and marvellous people and anyway what's wrong with Max Boyce and S4C?

Who Hates Who in international rugby

If music be the language of love, then rugby must be the language of hate. There is a sophisticated and unbending list of opposed nations that all supporters must respect and uphold. The problem is, to speak the language of hate you have to understand these rules. In brief these may be laid down as follows:

No-one hates the Irish. Except the Welsh. Who hate everyone. Excluding the Welsh. The Scottish hate the English. And the Welsh. But especially the English. Everyone hates the English. Including the English themselves. The French are only interested in money. And hate the English because of Joan of Arc. Everyone hates the All Blacks, although they sneakingly admire them. Everyone loves South Africa because they never play anyone, therefore they never beat anyone. For some reason they are still always rumoured to be the best. Papua New Guinea hate the English. The Pitcairn Islands hate the English. The Germans don't play rugby but if they did they would hate the English as well.

Despite the immense hatred burning up inside rival fans there is never any violence among rugby supporters. The only way a rugby fan can express his dislike of his fellow fan is by singing louder than him and/or by drinking more than him before the game. Which is a very tenuous excuse for getting drunk, but since when has that ever really mattered?

Rugby fans don't throw anything, kick anything, vandalise anything, or indeed leave any mark at all where they have been. The only evidence that a train has been taken over by rugby fans is normally a mountain of empty beer cans in the buffet car or alternatively no beer cans at all if it is an unattractive fixture. Rugby fans who do kick, throw, vandalize or molest are usually called 'not real fans' and are labelled 'football fans out for a bit of trouble'.

Other uses for a set of rugby posts

A useful source of cash is often neglected by many financially hard pressed clubs. Below are four simple schemes to hire out the rugby posts and generate a useful income for the small club.

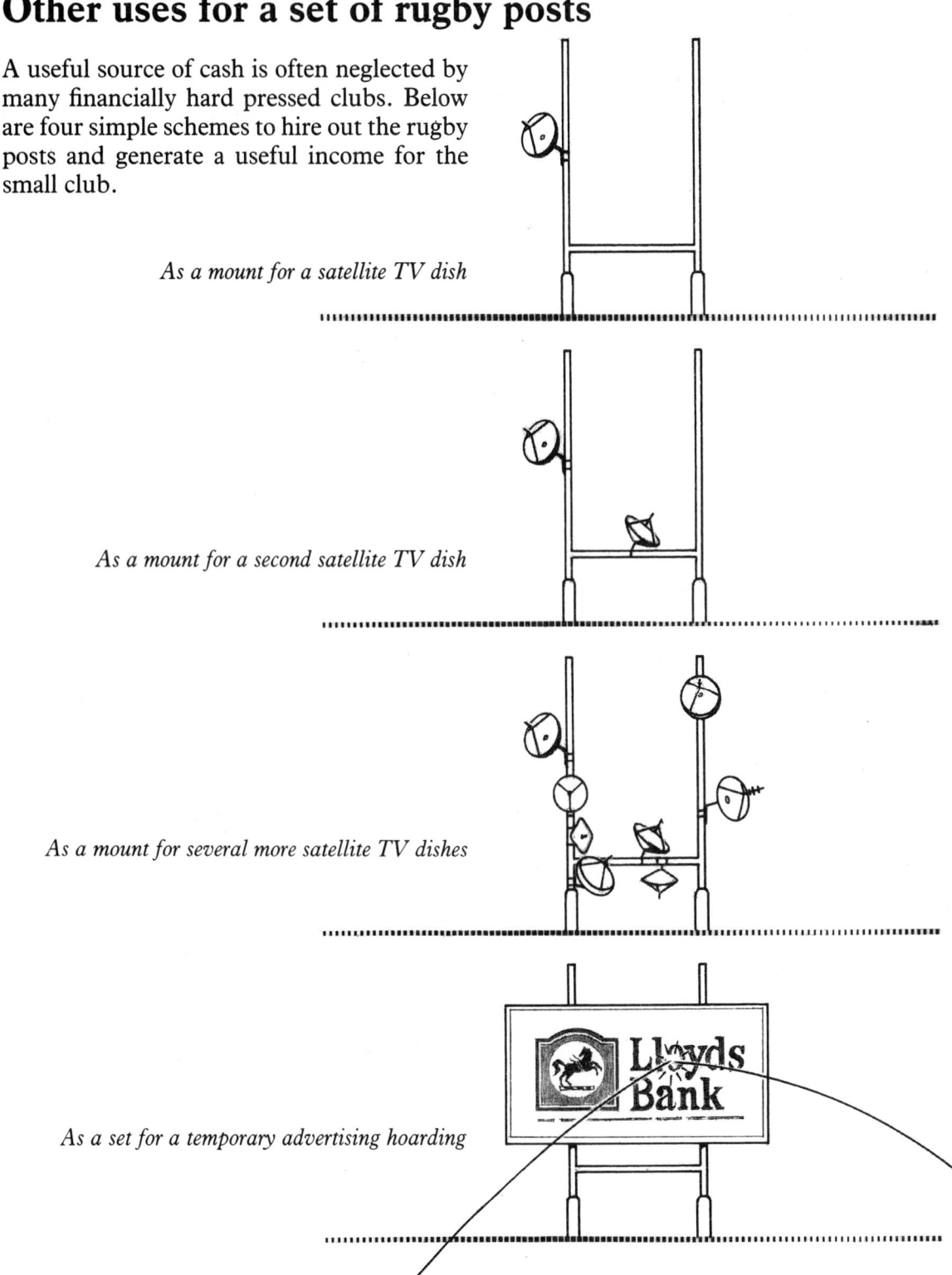

As a mount for a satellite TV dish

As a mount for a second satellite TV dish

As a mount for several more satellite TV dishes

As a set for a temporary advertising hoarding

Rugby as she is sung

Few sports exercise the vocal chords more than rugby. Even non-Welshmen can usually raise a bawdy song or two in the clubroom bar on a Saturday night and the rugby song itself has drifted into common folklore.

It is not well appreciated, however, that many well-known songwriters have looked towards rugby for their inspiration, and in an effort to broaden the song sheet and offer some well-needed variety to the contemporary songbook I have included below a few of the less well-known rugby songs.

'I Ain't Goin' Down To Rosslyn Park No More'

BOB DYLAN

(*accompanied by a guitar*)

Went down to Rosslyn Park
To watch those Harlequins play
Took me some coffee
and a bar of Milky Way.

I clapped and I cheered every time
the ball went to a Harlequin
I said if they can just work it out
to the flanks then they can win.

But they went down 79–2
to a depleted Vale of Lune.
It's the last time I'm going there
on a Saturday afternoon.

(HARMONICA BREAK)

No I ain't never going back
Never goin' back to Rosslyn Park no more.
No I ain't never going back,
to Rosslyn Park that's for sure.

'I'm In The Mood For Hooking'

THE NOLAN SISTERS

(*disco beat*)

I'm in the mood for hooking
And loose rucking
Feel like scrumming the night away

I'm in the mood for locking
And for blocking
Feel like trying the overlap

Rugby
Rugby has got me
Just show me your loose balls
and nothing can a-stop me!

'The Leader of the Pack'

THE RONNETTES

(*traditional; new lyrics: Gareth Edwards*)

I met him at the National Trials
He turned around and held me off
You get the picture
Yes we see
That's when I fell for the Leader of the
    Pack.

I felt so helpless what could I do do do
He grabbed my neck until I turned blue
I said d'you think you could perhaps let go
He tied my legs up in a double bow
I'll never forget you
Leader of the Pack.

'Anarchy in the Five Nations'

THE SEX PISTOLS

(*punk*)

We don't need no national selectors
We don't need no gum protectors
We don't need no ten-yard rule
We don't need no national pool

All we need is lots of punching
Arm locks flying, tackles crunching
All we want is lots of fighting
Lots of putting the boot right in

Anarchy in the five nations
Anarchy in the five nations
Anarchy in the five nations
Anarchy in the five nations

Clean rugby songs

Rugby songs are a part of the game but just occasionally in mixed or sensitive company it may be necessary to temper down the songs and soften the language. A pleasant tea dance or concert party can be rudely spoilt by an unwitting rugby player taking the stage to perform his bawdy piece without realising the offence it will cause.

In order that followers can still enjoy a robust sing-song without offending their guests a new 'all-clean' version of the traditional rugby songbook has just been published (Prudish Publications £1.99) for which I was asked to write the sleeve notes and for which I consequently wrote something off the cuff. Among selections to be found in that publication are the following:

MY FAVOURITE CLEAN RUGBY
   SONGBOOK

Two German officers crossed the Rhine ta-
   boo ta-boo
Two German officers crossed the Rhina ta-
   boo ta-boo
Two German officers crossed the Rhine ta-
   boo ta-boo
They were polite to the women and didn't
   drink any wine.

———

T'was on the good ship *Venus*
By God you should have seen us
The figurehead was very respectable
And so was the first mate as well.

———

Four and twenty virgins
Came down from Inverness
And when the ball was over
They went back to Inverness (as virgins).

Singing hello to your father
Hello to the wall
If you've never been out
On a Saturday night
You've never been out at all.

The vicar's daughter she was there
thrilling them to bits
serving up the fresh fruit cup
and lots of tasty bits.

———

If I was the marrying kind
Which thank the Lord I'm not sir
The kind of girl that I would wed
Would be very sensible and correct and not
   at all flighty.

———

Autographs

One of the lesser-known perils of rugby stardom is the frequency with which one is asked to sign rugby balls. Charity functions, testimonials, man of the match balls, the top flight player's pen is never rested. A few tips learnt over the years might help the novice signer.

Firstly, never attempt to sign a ball whilst it is still in flight. It is practically impossible to sign a moving ball and can only end in a nasty injury as you try to remove the ballpoint tip from up your nose.

Secondly, remember the purpose of your signature is simply to add a personal touch and not to engage in an elaborate piece of decoration. It is futile to spend several hours intricately engraving your name in copper plate on the ball surface, or to add a gothic interpretation with flowery water nymphs and bathing cherubs surrounding your signature.

Thirdly, always make sure the ball is well supported when you sign it. Rugby balls have a nasty habit of rocking about when you put a pen to them and a moment's thought can save the embarrassment of handing back a badly blotched ball with an ugly ink blot where your name should have been.

And, for heaven's sake, remember to use a conventional blue or green ink when signing.

The use of luminous pink or fluorescent lemon may indeed say something about you but it is highly unlikely to be complimentary. Above all, resist any exotic desire to seal your oath by signing in blood.

Finally, and this may seem an obvious tip, but do make sure you know your own name. This doesn't normally present a problem but after a tired and emotional night celebrating it can take quite an effort to remember your own name. If in doubt get someone else to sign in your absence or offer to sign the ball next morning when you have sobered up. This will avoid the rudery of handing back a ball on which you have had to cross out several initial attempts before getting your name right.

More recently the craze has been for more exotic signatures. Or rather signatures on more exotic locations. This no doubt adds value to the article as signed balls must be two-a-penny by now, though the craze isn't without its complications. The advice is simply to take great caution and prepare carefully. Above all, never attempt to sign a fellow player's jock strap, especially whilst it is still being worn, and especially if you haven't warned him first.

10
THE REFEREE

Referees

The one rule of rugby (see elsewhere in this book) is that no-one on or off the field knows the exact rules of the game and that referees are no different in this respect. Where they are different is that unlike everyone else on the pitch, their decision actually counts.

For this reason the same game refereed by two different refs can have wildly differing outcomes. And since the profession attracts a wide number of eccentrics, the permutation of outcomes can be as wide as these eccentricities.

The question then is really how, and why, these refs are appointed. The *how* part is the job of the National and International Selection Panel. An unknown group of men who are rumoured to appoint, and less frequently un-appoint the game's refs. No-one knows who these men are. They themselves may be unaware of their duties for all we know. The job is never advertised in the press nor does it ever appear in a Jobcentre window. These men appear to operate with all the secrecy of the Masons or the Magic Circle, and generally generate the same lack of public respect and suspicion as these former two inspire.

More relevant then is the question *why?* Why should a man give up his Saturday afternoons for six months of the year to have insults and abuse hurled at him for his pains?

1 Sadism
A good many refs go on the game simply to satisfy their perverse longing for inflicting pain. Seeing others suffer is their 'bag' and the rugby field offers ample opportunities. The ten-yard rule was invented solely to pamper their whim and allow them the pleasure of seeing grown men grovel.

2 Masochism
Perversely, those interested in inflicting pain on themselves are also likely to be attracted to the refs' world where a timorous or weak man in charge can suffer mental and physical pain that would be hard to equal. The thought of being liplashed by thirty bruisers on a cold and windswept peat bog sends a thrill of delight down their backs and makes them give up their precious weekends for an afternoon's assault and battery.

3 Loneliness
Surprisingly some men take up refereeing for the camaraderie and fellowship it brings; the idea being that instead of a lonely Saturday at home you can spend it in the jocular company

of a bunch of hearty rugby players. This neglects the fact that for the time the ref shares their company he is their sworn enemy and likely to feel as lonely as it is possible to feel.

4 The uniform

Refereeing attracts those drawn to authority and discipline. You're not likely to see too many long hairy kaftan-wearing hippy drop-outs pulling on the ref's gear, but a part-time traffic warden who happens to be an auxiliary police officer and a member of the TA, and chairman of the local Neighbourhood Watch is a prime candidate. These men regard the ref's job as a duty and see themselves as the gallant few sent to uphold law and order.

5 Those who can't . . .

The old adage of those who can do, those who can't . . . holds very true in rugby where the obvious next port of call for the reject player is the ref's changing room. The striking anomaly here is that from not being able to get a place in the team the reject player now finds himself holding the most crucial position on the pitch. Thus players who would mock the inabilities of a teammate and scorn him in training suddenly find they are obeying his whistle on the pitch.

6 The keen

There is a small intake of refs each year who believe it or not genuinely enjoy the job and see it very nearly as an art form. They study refereeing, discuss it with other refs, and arrange conferences where they can meet with other refs and talk far into the night about the new Rule 34B. The keen ref regards the game as ancillary to his work, a sort of tapestry about which he can weave his picture. In his eyes the referee doesn't simply referee a game, he controls it, orchestrates it, defines its ebb and flow, is the master craftsman who single-handedly makes it happen.

7 The form master

Obviously this is restricted to schools games or matches against school opponents. The problem is that in these games the referee is in a position of artificial superiority. True, the ordinary ref can send a player off and report him to the RFU but there it stops. The schoolteacher ref can threaten detention, extra prep, reports to the headmaster, even expulsion from the school. The result is a game in which the teams cower from the ref and are scared to appeal in case it brings extra homework. The crunch comes in the annual old boys' match when this megapower no longer applies, at least to the old boys' side. Years of subjugation usually boil over with the ref called the vilest names under the sun, being verbally slaughtered and laid to the cross for the full eighty minutes.

8 The sixteenth man

This is an oddity that only occurs where the official ref fails to appear. In these cases, the sixteenth man from one side is usually volunteered to run the game. The result is as biased a contest as you could witness. The usual form, therefore, is to split the match with the sixteenth man from each side running forty minutes each. The cheatery of the first half is thus compensated for by the equally one-sided reffing in the second. Teams who might be unfairly down 36–0 suddenly stage a remarkable comeback in the second half scoring tries from knocked-on forward passes that ran out of touch three times and were touched down a good six feet from the line.

Referee's report

The one source of revenge, and it is a rich one, comes in the ref's report. This is the report filled in by both captains in which they report on and mark the ref's performance. In such ways the mistreated teams have, literally, the last word. However, it again brings a slight problem since the intention is that good refs are promoted on merit and bad refs not.

Unfortunately, in the lowest divisions, this simply means the bad ref stays where he is and it is likely everyone will cop for them again next season. Self interest here suggests the best policy therefore is to give glowing reports to the bad refs in the hope that they will be promoted up into another league, and thus out of your hair, while the good refs gets a total panning and are thus around next time.

The eventual outcome of all this is a situation where the bad ref is continually promoted up through the ranks in a bid to be rid of him till the point that he receives his international card and inflicts his awfulness on the five nations. It is clearly a cruel trick to play on our national team but where the alternative is another season of miserable refereeing then drastic measures are required.

The rules of rugby

The Shorter Rulebook

(abridged from *The Longer Rulebook* by leaving a few of the longer, boring ones out)

1   There are no rules of rugby.
2   The only rules of rugby that may be construed to be rules are those rules that may be construed to be rules at the time of their being construed by the officials.
3   Any rule that is construed to be a rule by the fact of it being called a rule by an official may be immediately contradicted by a second rule by the said same official.
4   No official need be called upon to explain any rule or to defend any decision he may make based upon a non-existent ruling, and should he choose to so explain his actions his explanation cannot be used as evidence against him.
5   No official may make up more than fifty new rules in any one game without prior permission from the RFU. (This is not actually a rule and can, therefore, be ignored as irrelevant.)
6   Any official who finds he or she is out of breath and unable to keep up with play may, if he or she so wishes, blow their whistle to call back play in order that they might catch breath for a few seconds.
7   Any official who finds he or she is more fit than both teams may, should they so wish, be permitted to allow play to continue uninterrupted without a break until both teams drop and beg for a breather, at which point the official may refuse to blow the whistle and wave play on.
8   An amendment shall be written into the Full Rules of the Game to the effect that 'the Offside Ruling shall be totally incomprehensible to all players and officials alike and shall be employed at whim by the officials as and when they see fit'.
9   Where an official is found to be unfit through drink it shall be the duty of both teams immediately to say nothing about it to anyone.
10   Rule 10 shall, in future, be known as rule 8, which will itself be known as Rule 4. Rule 2 will be known as Rule 6, while Rule 7 and Rule 9 will become Rule 1 and Rule 5 respectively. The new Rule 4 will then be swapped with the former Rule 2, to become

Rules 14 and 27, while Rules 2, 8, 4, 6, 7 and 32 will be re-numbered 1, 2, 7, 6 and 4, although not necessarily in that order. Rule 3 will remain unchanged. The purpose of these changes is to further confuse the player and make it impossible for anyone to know what is going on.

11   Will remain as Rule 11 although no-one will be quite sure what it is about. (See Rule 11.)

12   Where a rule has been amended by reason of an amendment, an amending rule to that effect shall be appended to the amendment and shall be deemed an appending amendment to an amended appendment and shall be amended accordingly.

The Abridged Shorter Rulebook

1   There are no rules of rugby.

You are the ref . . .

This is your chance to referee a rugby game. Below are ten common problems you might face on the rugby pitch. Write down your answers, then check against the correct answers given below.

1   A dog races on to the pitch, picks the ball up in its teeth, runs fifty yards down the pitch evading all tackles and drops the ball in the try area. What should you do?

2   A conversion attempt comes down on top of one of the goalposts. The ball is spiked by the post and lodges firmly on top of the post. What do you do?

3   Both teams turn up for the game in the same strip. No alternatives can be found and no way of identifying the two sides can be arranged. What should you do?

4   You can't find a coin to toss up for ends and it's wet and windy and you feel a cold coming on and you only agreed to referee because a friend twisted your arm. What should you do?

5   One of the team captains is your boss at work and quite clearly grounds the ball

before claiming a try. What is your decision?

6   A female streaker runs on to the pitch and proceeds to run up and down the pitch with no clothes on. What should you do?

7   The goalkeeper catches the ball on his goalline near the edge of the penalty box. Aware he can only move four steps, he dribbles the ball outside the box then re-enters the penalty box, picks up the ball, and kicks it down field. What should you do?

8   At a scrum the whole front row of one team break wind in unison together. The effect causes the other team to loose concentration and concede a try. What do you do?

9   A fullback picks up a loose ball on his own goalline. He jinxes inside, sidesteps a tackle, sidesteps another tackle, avoids a head lock, passes to the scrum half who passes inside to the wing threequarters who feeds it across field to the prop, he jinxes, sidesteps, hands off another tackle, and feeds the fullback who dum-

mies, jinxes, runs thirty yards, sends a forty-yard pass, runs into space for the return and makes a fifty-yard sprint to the line. What do you do?

10 At a line-out you notice a player from one team grab hold of an opponent's goolies and give them a twist. What should you do?

Answers

1 Tell the dog's owner to send it to the next England trial.

2 Abandon the match and call it a draw and go home.

3 Abandon the match and call it a draw and go home.

4 Abandon the match and call it a draw and go home.

5 You must ignore all personal interest and make a decision based purely on what you see. Obviously, if it is worth five thousand pounds a year and a new company car then what you should have seen was a perfectly legal try.

6 Nothing. Who wants to be a killjoy?

7 Check you are in the right game. It sounds to me like you've wandered on to a neighbouring football pitch.

8 Try and book them as the cabaret for the annual rugby club dinner, they sound just the sort of thing that's needed to liven things up.

9 Sit down for five minutes for a rest.

10 Be grateful it's not you.

How did you do?

All ten right and you have clearly been cheating and peeped at the answers. I don't know about rugby but if you ever go into used car sales or estate agency you should do very well.

Five to nine answers right: good, you are either very well up on the rules of the game or are a moderately good cheat who peeps some of the time but then feels a bit guilty. Over-come the guilt and you should do very well.

One to five answers right: not bad but you clearly get worried in case someone comes in and catches you peeping. Either brush up on the laws or try to improve your cheating. There is no point cheating a little bit. If you're going to do it then hang everything and go for broke.

None: national county championship standard.

II

KIT

Security

In recent years there has been an alarming increase in crime from rugby changing rooms. And this crime has not been restricted to valuable possessions either. Light-fingered thieves will make off with practically anything left unattended and to combat this crime wave a number of security measures are now recommended for protecting a player's kit.

Gum shields

Gum shields can be marked with indelible ink which makes them conspicuous and easy to trace. Try ordinary household enamel. A bright or distinctive gum shield in orange and purple stripes is easily recognisable and hence of little value to the thief. Another technique is to attach a small eye hook to your gum shield so that a chain may be attached to the shield when not in the mouth. This chain can then be affixed to a permanent object like a radiator or bicycle rack by means of a small padlock. It is advisable to check with the owner of any property to which one intends affixing a gum shield in this way. While most people will not object, it can cause alarm and distress if no warning has been given. Alternatively you could try a proprietary gum trap.

In normal use these look and operate like a normal shield but they are equipped with a small concealed switch that causes the shield to clamp shut like a mousetrap in a bogus mouth, trapping the tongue and rendering the jawbone rigid.

Jock straps

Jock strap rustling has become a serious menace in many pavilions in recent months and has caused the authorities to look at several solutions. Among those now recommended are:

- **Alarm devices**
  A small alarm device can now be attached to the outside of the jock strap and emits a loud, high-pitched wail if worn by another player. Apart from attracting attention, the shock can cause temporary disablement and even paralysis of the groin.

- **Genetic marking**
  Scientists have now found a way of detecting the crutch marks in a jock strap in much the same way as fingerprints are taken. Eventually a central record of all jock straps and their respective crutch marks should be available and a quick and effective check procedure made possible.

- **Scented jock straps**
  By coating the jock strap in a strong or distinctive perfume it is made less attractive to the casual thief who seeks anonymity for his crime. A jock strap stained with a ladies' perfume or toilet water is far less likely to be stolen than a non-smelling version; and whilst it may prove slightly offensive to some players, especially front row prop forwards, it is a simple and effective security measure. (NB: My preferred brand is Chanel No.5.)

Rugby as she is changed

Other sports have to undergo hardships and privations as severe or worse than rugby but few seem to revel in the discomfort quite so much as rugby. And nowhere is this more so than in the vexed question of changing rooms. The game is legend with colourful stories of the rugby players' changing plight, each one positively wallowing in its own awfulness.

In truth, rugby suffers no worse than any other sport. True there are converted railway carriages, even unconverted railway carriages, still in service with the backwoodsmen of the rugby community, reminders that survive to validate those stories of the changers' woe. But more often the truth is of passably anonymous modern brick stumps set in the centre of a vast corporation wasteland. They are clean, warm and boast hot water. The rugby player should be glad of the comforts they provide. Yet, strangely, it is the passing of the Lower Piddlinghaven cowshed and the demise of the roofless tin shed of the Oxenthistlemoor club that many players regret most.

Many players would give their left arm to once more be allowed to change behind a hedge or in the back seat of the captain's car. Fond eyes will glaze over with mist as memories of the time the team changed in the snug bar of the local pub for a game in the sticks of Norfolk. Even international players, blessed with all the facilities of Twickenham, would secretly swap their all for the chance to strip off in the back of that derelict cattle truck in the bethistled corner of a small paddock where their first encounter with the game began.

So it is with them in mind that I list below a few home discomforts that can be re-introduced to the sanitised dressing rooms of the eighties in a bid to keep nostalgia alive:

1   Sheep
No dressing room is complete without a few sheep to wander aimlessly in and out.

2   Wind
This is essential if your dressing room is to bring back memories. Try a professional wind machine or a dozen fan heaters with the heating element taken out.

3   Dirt
A vital ingredient of all this fond nostalgia was dirt. A team changing in a pig shed would come out looking as though they had just played a full game rather than were about to commence. Try keeping a herd of cows in the changing rooms before matches or wash the walls down with raw sewage.

4   Impropriety
Most bygone changing arrangements demanded a certain amount of immodesty. It was accepted that a certain poundage of raw flesh would be on public view and was a part of the charm. Try opening any windows and removing any curtains or gauze. If necessary, construct a line of mirrors to reflect the on-

goings (or rather off-goings) in the changing room to the passing public.

5 Water

Water plays a great part in primitive changing rooms. It came in through the roof. It came in through the floor. It came in through the windows. And it came in in buckets. Always swill the floor of the changing room out with cold water before entering and continue to swill out as you get changed. Arrange a rota if necessary. Try to fix up a sprinkler hose in the centre of the room and leave any taps running.

6 Lack of water

By perversity, there should never be any water available for washing after the game. Provide a small pail of tepid rainwater and a bar of encrusted carbolic and instruct players they must use nothing else.

7 Hooks

To create an authentic feel of the past all hooks should be removed and a series of rusty nails driven into the walls in their place. Make sure these are bent downwards to ensure all clothing slips off and on to the wet floor at the vital moment that the last garment is added. Alternatively, provide no nails at all so the clothes have to be left in a screwed up bundle resting on the players' shoes.

8 Space

The one thing that was never available to the primitive changer was space. Fifteen players would be crammed into a four by eight hut, three to a hook (see above) with a 20 watt light bulb to illuminate the darkness. To recreate the bonhomie of this world, players should cordon off three-quarters of the modern changing room and squeeze themselves into the remaining corner. Board up all windows and switch off the light for that final touch.

Players who take these steps will find they are in their own heaven and will lapse into a state of blissful reminiscence.

New tracksuits

A little known, yet often serious, problem facing the rugby player is the peril of the new tracksuit. The rugby player's on-pitch wardrobe is still locked in a perpetual timewarp where socks were expected to last a lifetime, and shorts even longer.

What other sport, for instance, can boast a style of shorts unchanged from the fifties and still with a little pocket at the front? Come to that, what other sport wants to boast shorts with pockets? They serve no useful purpose, a legacy of a past era when players might take keys, wallet, even a pocket handkerchief on the pitch with them.

In this world of bygone fashion, the quality of the rugby player's kit thus matters little, and indeed the more threadbare and bleached an item the more respect it commands. Rather like a war wound, wear and tear boasts of a glorious past and is exhibited with pride and passion.

And nowhere does this tradition hold truer than in the case of tracksuits. A worn, torn, faded and jaded tracksuit speaks volumes of a player, while a neat, new example can yield the reverse and provoke only scorn.

It is like a new blazer and satchel at school. Like the new boy at school shamed by his new uniform, the player in a new tracksuit finds the same shame and embarrassment waiting for him.

But tracksuits do eventually die, and much

as one might stitch and darn there comes a point when they can carry on no longer. Here is where ingenuity is required.

Start by soaking your tracksuit in a solution of three parts water, to one part lime cement (where cement is unavailable, any building produce will do). The effect is to take off the newness. Other things that may be added include soil, raw manure, nitric acid, bleach, grease, sour milk and beer. Leave the tracksuit to soak for two to three days, then rinse thoroughly and repeat. Continue to repeat until the tracksuit is as faded and shapeless as the wearer.

Another technique is to use the tracksuit as makeshift car mats for a few weeks. Or put them in the dog's basket for a couple of months. Or put them in the washing machine with a bag of nails and switch them on to spin.

Finally, if all this doesn't work then find a piece of mud and roll around in it in the tracksuit for several hours. Try and find somewhere that is secluded. Remember, you are doing this so you won't look out of place on the training pitch and if half the neighbourhood sees you behaving like a beached whale then your bid for normality and acceptance may be thwarted.

Repeat the above procedures for any other new kit that may be purchased.

Velcro

In a game where body contact counts for so much I find it surprising that no leading player has yet discovered the enormous advantages that Velcro offers the nimble-footed fortune seeker.

Velcro, you will remember, is the stuff of a thousand quick change routines, and, with sticky backed plastic, is one of this country's major institutions. The technique is simple. Two strips of Velcro are placed together to secure a fixing. To break the bond you simply pull the two pieces apart and hey presto a clean, re-sealable break.

Imagine the virtues of this for the player wishing to evade a tackle. A shirt held together with Velcro would simply pull apart under the grab of a tackler's grasp and free the wearer to continue his run. Shorts designed to split in the same way might be jettisoned at the hands of hapless pursuers. In short, a player prepared to dress from top to toe in a Velcro-ised kit would have enormous escapological advantages over his opponents. And once his try is made he may jog back and pick up his discarded clothing and re-assemble it ready to be put back on and worn again.

The beauty is there is nothing at all in the rules of rugby to prevent such a kit being worn. Indeed at no point in the rules of the game is the subject of Velcro even mentioned.

Of course the disadvantages of a Velcro rugby kit are not difficult to see. It demands that a player be willing to shed part or all of his clothing in the name of victory. (A Velcroed jock strap is possible though decency would normally draw the line here. Such rank exhibitionism is likely to get tongues wagging in the changing room.)

But for the player wishing to radically improve his game at a stroke my advice is simply to spend a night with a strip of Velcro and a sewing machine adapting your kit as described above.

It may not get you that long-awaited England call-up but it will improve your points average dramatically, plus it will provide valuable work experience should you ever want to seek work as a male stripper.

12

MUD

How to recognise a fellow player in the mud

In games that develop into a muddy fracas and mess it often becomes increasingly difficult to distinguish fellow players. This is not altogether a disaster. In such conditions it is unlikely any real progress will be made and passing the ball to friend or foe alike will end up with much the same conclusion: stalemate.

Nonetheless there are occasions when it would be useful to have a quick and ready means of identifying allies in the quagmire. Perhaps the most promising of these would be some coded signal transmitted constantly, inaudible to other ears but instantly recognisable to players of your own team. After all, dolphins seem capable of such a form of communication so why shouldn't rugby players, only marginally less gifted, be so able?

Unfortunately, short of strapping a dolphin to your back and allowing him to guide you, there seems little to profit from this example. So for the more practically minded the following are suggested:

1 Flares

The lighted kind, as opposed to the worn type. Distinctive coloured flares let off at crucial moments can pinpoint your fellow team members, plus the effect of a passing movement combined with simultaneously ignited flares can be quite impressive; rather like a Red Arrow air display. Incidentally, worn flares can also be used to identify your team in the mud, although the effect of heavily soiled flares can be debilitating because of their vast surface area.

2 Duck calls

If all the players are equipped with duck calls before the game, identification becomes simply a case of quacking one's duck call constantly throughout the game. The technique has the advantage of cheapness and simplicity. The disadvantage is you may attrack a flock of Canada geese or worse still a flock of hunters with loaded rifles to aim at you. Worth considering all the same.

3 Radio pagers

An alternative use for the humble radio pager. The disadvantage is that rushing off to find a phone box to call in and collect your message can upset the flow of any move, and other phone users are likely to become irate and frustrated if they have to wait behind a line of soggy, sweaty rugby players to make a phone call.

4   A gimmick

An easily recognisable gimmick or joke trick may be one answer. A joke 'arrow-through-the-head' or a silly false nose may make you and your fellows in grime identifiable even when coated in a thick covering of mud. The advantage is that you can still operate as a team. The disadvantage is that you are likely to become the laughing stock of the district if your photograph appears in the local paper. (You may very well be this already so that might not be such a problem.)

5   Body language

One of the phenomena of social research over the last twenty years has been the rise in the study of body language and the messages we transmit through our gestures and postures. Often these can be subtle and slight and readable only by the informed. There is an opportunity here that rugby players may well be able to exploit. Try to devise a series of simple body motions that your fellow players can read and understand: a wink, a frown, a nod, a slight cough, all can be telling to the initiated. Be careful not to over-exaggerate, rubbing one's thigh provocatively and moaning in a deep voice as you go down for a scrum is not likely to go down well with opponents. If it does then you really are in trouble.

6   Sixth sense is another powerful weapon

Players able to read each other's minds can be a rare bonus on a muddy pitch. It is often claimed identical twins hold this power, and triplets likewise. Any woman who gives birth to the first set of identical demi-quintuplets (fifteen identical children) holds the key to rugby dominance for the next twenty years. If you are interested, check with your local hospital gynaecology unit. Otherwise it might be worth scouting round the personal ads in the psychic and clairvoyant magazines. Remember a useful medium doesn't necessarily make a good player – crystal balls and rugby balls being quite distinct – and it is wise to arrange a trial before selection.

7   Smell

Always a potent device. The same after shave is one possible solution, though the risk is your opponents may have used it as well. It is therefore more sensible to go for a more obscure aroma. Try a ladies' perfume or toilet water. It is likely to make you quite recognisable. Remember it is difficult to remove perfume aroma afterwards so you should avoid travelling home from the game on public transport. Another possible aroma is a distinct food. Strong cheese is one particularly good example. If a team rub themselves all over with a stiff blue Stilton before the game it is quite likely the smell will remain with them for the full eighty minutes. Do explain your actions if you are sharing the changing rooms with another team; it can be distressing watching another man use cheese as a body rub.

8   Drunkenness

A team that takes to the field in a state of obvious drunkenness is likely to be quite recognisable (although not always by themselves). This is not a particularly good way of overcoming the problem of mud, but is a very good excuse for a drinking session before the match.

The Rugby League end-of-play strip guide

Most supporters can identify their own team at the start of play. But this handy guide lets you spot your own team's players in those vital last few minutes of play.

Castleford   Salford   Dewsbury   Doncaster   Wigan

St Helen's   Widnes   Hunslet   Barrow   Featherstone

Hull   Hull KR   Bradford   Leeds   Workington

Oldham   Rochdale   Halifax   Wakefield   Warrington

Keighley   York   Runcorn   Swinton   Whitehaven

Batley   Leigh   Mansfield   Sheffield   Huddersfield

Mud: the universal leveller

Mud is the great democracy of rugby, the universal leveller, the one true feature by which all players are united; young and old, swift and slow, beginner and England star, everyone is united by mud.

It respects no man more than the next and is classless in its assault. That is why it is so important to the game for without it rugby could not claim its position as the first socialist sport.

So it is odd that until recently Russia, of all the world's nations, should not have embraced it and taken the sport to its bosom. After all it embodies all that is noble in the communist cause: equality, unity and hard, earnest, honest graft.

Why then this anomaly? Russian rugby has at last taken its position on the world stage, the spirit of *glasnost* helping to break down the barriers and foster a capable national squad, but until this belated arrival its contribution to Russian sporting history was notably unnotable.

A brief history of Russian rugby

1917
No mention of rugby by Lenin as he addresses the workers in St Peter's Square at the start of the communist revolution.

1937
Height of Stalin's purges. Many millions sent to death in Siberia. No mention at all of rugby.

1941
Russia enters the war (no mention of rugby).

1945
End of Second World War and formation of the Warsaw Pact. Birth of modern Europe and the polemic division between East and West, but absolutely no mention at all of rugby.

1962
Cuban missile crisis. Khruschev and Kennedy at loggerheads over missiles and the Cold War at its height. Rugby still not mentioned.

1964
Brezhnev takes over as First Secretary. Adopts a rapprochement policy with the United States but doesn't mention rugby.

1985
Gorbachev now in power. Political and economic reforms underway but still no mention whatsoever of rugby.

13
TOURING

Touring

Touring forms an important part of many players' calendars. In fact for most players it forms the only important part. It provides a glorious, totally legitimate excuse to leave wife and family behind and enjoy a seven-day, round-the-clock drinking marathon whose excesses are broken only by the occasional bout of rugby.

Moreover, since one is surrounded by a coachful of equally hell-minded compatriots, there is no peer pressure to conform and the normal laws of human behaviour that might apply to you as an individual are revoked.

Players who have spent the entire season being kicked from twenty-five yard line to twenty-five yard line realise why they have put up with six months of suffering when the annual tour dates are announced. Grown men have been known to cry and kiss the ground as they board the coach at the start of their week-long drinking orgy. Even the player who last year had his entire belongings emptied from the coach windows on the elevated section of the M4 and was forced to spend the entire tour in the shirt and trousers he turned up in, allows himself a mental jig of excitement when his name appears on the tour sheet.

You should be careful then to respect this sacred week and to obey the conventions on which it has rested. In particular you should be certain not to take certain objects with you on tour.

NOT allowed on rugby tours:

- ◼ your family
- ◼ a diary (could be dangerous and used as evidence when you arrive home)
- ◼ anything that looks like mineral water
- ◼ milk (except in the form of Mars Bars; standard diet on most club tours)
- ◼ a special homeopathic aromatic pillow (it may be ideal for curing a stiff neck but in the presence of a crowd of rugby rowdies it is a definite no no)
- ◼ a pair of Postman Pat pyjamas (even if they do make them in your size and you always sleep in them at home. Remember you will have to live with the caustic comments on the contents of your suitcase for the next ten seasons)
- ◼ a thermos and travel rug (unlikely to get past the first service stop without being ceremoniously dumped in a waste bin by your teammates)

- an itinerary (most tours involve confusion and muddling, along the lines of 'we played here last year and I'm sure it was just next to a council estate', or 'all we need to do is find that funny junction with the pub on the corner and we can find it from there')
- boots (at least one person should forget his boots and have to play all five games in trainers or pumps)
- a coaching manual (perish the coach who thought it would be a good opportunity to get some extra coaching in ahead of next season)
- a coach (motor, or the other. At some point in the tour the team bus and the team coach are to go missing – the former by accident, the latter on purpose.)
- a driver (at some point in the tour the driver will be required by convention to go missing leaving the players to negotiate the trip to the next match by public transport)
- any identifiable papers (rather like foreign agents it is essential that all members on the tour travel incognito and cannot be identified in the event of arrest lest relatives back home be alerted and get wind of events)
- anyone who is there for the rugby

Mismatches

One of the perennial problems with the tour is the standard of opposition. Teams going back to old hunting grounds won't have too much trouble. Over the years a rare process of symbiosis takes place by which both teams seem to equalise out their standards to provide a reasonable match. Either that, or the fixture is simply not renewed. But where new tours start up the problem can become acute.

Not that I had first-hand knowledge of this affair till recent years when I started to drop down through the club ranks and found myself in less austere playing company. A gentle season of hacking through the less well-known pastures of minor rugby was coming to a close and a respite in sight when the team tour was announced to enthusiastic support. Alas, my vision of a pleasant week shaking off the season's injuries with a few pleasant friendlies was drastically misin-

formed and what promised to be a gentle knock around with some French village team suddenly turns out to be a needle match the host team must win at all costs. Either that, or the host team is so superior that it would be a physical impossibility for them to lose.

The first hint that something is amiss comes with your arrival in the town to discover the match has actually been advertised. Posters promoting Le Grand Match litter the town and suggest this may be more than the stroll you had envisaged.

You will allay your initial fears no doubt by the comfort of several large brandies and the thought that no-one in their right minds could possibly want to watch you play. After all, in England you have been pushed to raise a team, let alone supporters, every available free body being conscripted to the playing side. Why on earth then should anyone actually give up their Sunday afternoon to witness some cluttered clogging match.

But come the following morning your reassurances will be dashed cruelly. People will greet you in the street, talk of the match, ask your team plan, and worst of all, say they will be there. As more and more passers by stop to offer the same greeting you know your number is up. You try to search out the fixtures secretary to strangle him personally but he has gone into hiding.

At two o'clock you troop your way to the ground through a mass of cars and bystanders. The pavements throng with spectators, clapping you on the shoulders and offering well wishes.

It is too late to turn back. The honour of the club, admittedly never high, is at stake. You grin, you smile. You talk bravely of your own playing strengths and the weakness of the opposition. Neither of which you have any evidence to support. And it is now half past two and the changing room that should be a sea of merriment on tour is like a prison cell, fifteen anxious men, their faces pale and drawn, listening to a sound they have never heard before. It is the sound of a crowd, a real crowd, not just the fullback's girlfriend and a man exercising his dog.

By now the brandy from last night has reached your feet and is refusing to let them move. Your heart is pounding and you've been sat still for the last half hour. The pit of your stomach feels as though it is turning somersaults; your tongue feels as if it wants to shrink away and die; your mouth feels as if you have spent the day chewing polo mints in a heat wave, washed down only with tomato ketchup.

In a word, you feel terrible. The coach pokes his head out and announces there are five thousand out there. Then comes the most alarming news yet, they've paid!

This thought has never crossed your mind before. That someone should actually pay to watch you play is a totally new and alien concept. You would be pushed to raise any support at home if you paid *them,* and now people are actually handing over hard-won francs to watch this carnage on a foreign field.

You try to think up excuses: a bout of food poisoning; nettlerash; a prior engagement. It isn't working. There are five thousand people out there; if you skunk off now you will have let down your country.

And now it's five to three and you can hear the French pack going through their warm-up exercises. You haven't seen them yet and already they sound frightening. It is too late to turn back. Too late to claim it has all been some horrible mistake and that if your hosts don't mind you'll just slip back to the hotel and forget all about it. It is too late even for worrying. A brief moment of inner calm settles over the room – a sort of clearness of thought, a sanctity of mind. It must be the same calmness that soldiers experience when they go over the top to an almost certain death. Just as your team is about to do.

Now the French team are leaving the dressing room. You can hear their studs on the passageway outside. Even they sound frightening. Not like the normal studs that you have been used to; these studs sound cultured, athletic, co-ordinated. They sound like the studs of real players. And now it is your turn. The door opens. A French face pops his head round the jamb. 'We are ready, messieurs.' This is it! No more romps in the meadow with the occasional loose maul to contend with. This is it! The real thing. You are about to be catapulted from the ranks of the rank amateur at ease with his game, to the ranks of the total and absolute embarrassing failure.

You kiss your belongings – this might be the last time you see them – and troop out, making feeble attempts to prove your fitness by the odd leap and jump, nearly tripping over your shoelace and turning your ankle in the process.

Ninety minutes later it is all over. The battle is finished. The spoils decided: 123–0 wasn't a bad result considering. In fact once you got used to the speed and the energy you could feel quite at home. Of course it would still go down as a defeat in the record books, but in some ways you could see it as a victory. No-one actually cried, or ran and hid, or refused to come out after half time. And there was a point where you actually reached your opponents' twenty-five yard line and had you not fumbled that pass there is even a chance you might have got in sight of their line.

Admittedly the French had withdrawn their two best players on the hour and replaced them with fourteen-year-old schoolboys, and you had got the distinct impression that perhaps they weren't trying as hard in the scrum when they actually fed the ball through to you. But it was still a very fair result.

The crowd had seemed to enjoy themselves. Once they got used to the one-sided traffic, and the novelty of a try every two minutes had worn off, they settled down to a pleasant afternoon in the sun. Several seemed to start up picnics while a hardy crowd behind one goal took to cheering every time the Englishmen fielded the ball.

What's more no-one appeared to have asked for their money back or complained to the French officials about the mismatch. Indeed there was even talk of a re-match next year should the tour take place, with the French talking enthusiastically of an ideal outing for their under-eleven colts.

Those legs of jelly that had wobbled and knocked for the first half hour and had given way at the approach of any play, now feel the warm glow of genuine exercise, a feeling of having done their bit, a feeling that had never graced them before.

Afterwards, when the hugging and kissing was over and the crowd drifted away it was time to take stock. No, in hindsight, it was not the most balanced of fixtures. And the result would have to be hushed up and false accounts penned for relatives back home. And that group of French schoolboys who had gathered round the mini bus afterwards to laugh and jeer had somewhat taken the shine off the day. But it really wasn't all that bad an experience. Was it?

At home, on your sloping pitch, with the spring in one corner and the gusting wind behind your backs for both halves you might even have had a chance of holding them down to under a hundred. And who knows with training and exercise, and a little luck you might even make a match of it next year. Next year? Ah, the warm glow of post-match optimism.

Tour fixtures worth considering

Very often a team's name can be a guide to the standard of opposition you might expect to encounter. As a general rule the following are good examples of the types of teams you should try to take on:

■ Any team described as Old Boys. There are exceptions to this (e.g. Stewart's Mel FP) but an old boys' team from an unknown minor public school should generally be a reasonable bet.

- Any team described as Junior Colts, or less. Remember some fourteen year olds can be pretty nifty on their feet, but as a guiding principal physical intimidation in the changing rooms beforehand can soften up Colts, where an adult team would shrug it off, or indeed positively revel at the prospect of the conflict being stirred up.

- Any team below Third Fifteen. Remember major clubs may have a string of teams and their idea of a third fifteen may not exactly tally with your interpretation. Certainly by the time you reach the fifteenth fifteen of a club you have never heard of before and which appears to have trouble raising a literate fixtures secretary, let alone an able team, then you should be fairly safe.

- Any team that corresponds with you in green felt tip or whose fixtures secretary signs herself 'Mrs'. Again this is not a cardinal rule. Some very presentable clubs have appalling clerical standards and some women fixtures secretaries represent good clubs.

- Any team whose fixtures secretary writes a begging letter to you pleading to be let off the fixture because they can't raise a team.

- Any team that you have ever beaten previously or have seen take a humiliating defeat at the hands of a third-rate fifteen.

Unfortunately it is not really considered etiquette to write to possible opponents asking them to describe how bad they are. Besides, natural false modesty would no doubt persuade even the Harlequins' captain to write back falsely claiming his team were a weak and ill-trained crew who couldn't offer a decent match this time out.

Remember too that even if your opponents obey all of the criteria listed above you may still find yourself outclassed. The only really good way to take on a team you know you can beat is actually to hand pick your opponents' line-up yourself, and since few captains or selectors (with the exception of the England trial selectors; and how many times does the 'A' team come unstuck there?) enjoy this luxury, in the final toe punt your hopes must rest with the Gods.

The French and nudity

One of the great mysteries of the game of rugby is the French players' love of nudity. A foreign tour with a French party is less like a sporting event and more like a naturist's ramble.

The visiting French will frequently take off their clothes at the slightest opportunity, and often even where no opportunity presents itself: airport lounges, hotel lobbies, street bistros, nightclubs. All fall victim to the debagged Frenchman.

What should propel an entire nation of sportsmen to strip off in this way? Physique? Not really. While the average Frenchman is quite adequately endowed and owns a perfectly presentable body, they possess nothing that the rest of us don't own, and in roughly the same position and proportion. Sexuality? Again I doubt it. There is nothing particularly erogenous about fifty beefy rugby players standing in the queue at the duty-free desk with their trousers round their ankles. Is it then some call back to the past, a lost piece of body language? Doubtful too. Even in the distant historical past there is no record of exhibitionist behaviour. Take a look at the Bayeaux Tapestry, and I'll lay any odds you wish that there is not one case of mooning on it.

So what is the secret of such wanton trouserlessness? Perhaps it is a form of welcome. But if so, what form, and why does it only occur on rugby tours? French businessmen, to my knowledge, do not immediately drop their trousers on business tours abroad. President Mitterrand is not seen sans panteloons at foreign summits.

Perhaps it is a form of entertainment then, a gregarious act to greet guest hosts. But again there are other forms of entertainment that would prove just as suitable. Even on tours where there is a language barrier, it is surely easier to struggle with a phrase book to convey the warm glow of hospitality and bonhomie, rather than to lower one's pants to half mast and risk being misconstrued.

Or perhaps it is a release valve against suppression for the rest of the season. Once again doubtful. Certainly the French do not appear to drop their trousers when not on tour, but then neither do the rest of us. One could hardly say they were deprived men, forced against their will to cover up while playing on home soil.

No, the honest truth is there is no plausible reason. They are blatant trouser droppers and that is it. Some men lift shirts, the French drop their baggies. Tour with a French team and within minutes of arrival on foreign shores you can bet the pants will be down. And if you want to be a part of the squad then alas yours must come down too. There is little one can offer as comfort. Take heart from the fact that you will not be alone. Another twenty-eight buttocks will be shining alongside yours. And after a few days you will begin to lose the sense of shock and embarrassment that you felt first time round. Indeed you may even become blasé about the whole affair and become a confirmed trouser dropper yourself. This will be of no real value to you elsewhere in life, but it may make a useful titbit to throw in at dinner parties when the conversation is flagging or when struggling to find something to say when introduced to the Queen at a civic function; plus it is a handy aside to put down on your curriculum vitae when applying for jobs.

14

APPENDIX

The twilight years

The twilight years are made bearable only by the fact that the gradual loss of form and fitness is matched by an equal decline in one's ability to recognise this deterioration.

Thus the player embarking on his twilight seasons is able to convince himself that all is as it has always been and he is still at his sporting peak. He will not notice the yard or so dropped in speed, nor the sharp stabbing pain after every tackle. Nor will he notice the caustic comments traded at his expense or his slow slippage through the club ranks till he is bypassed by even the junior colts. In fact he will be blind to everything, adamant that any loss of athleticism is well countered by the accrued expertise and experience.

Even when he has been reduced to the occasional appearance in the sixth fifteen (and even then only as fill-in for a last minute absentee), he will be quite unfailing in his belief in his abilities.

Thus the cushion of the twilight years is kind and gentle, nature compensating for failing limbs with failing sight, helping to let the twilight player down as softly as possible. And by the time you have realised the dawning truth it is already way past the time when one can legitimately retire from the game and

the act of hanging one's boots up is less a trauma and more a relief. The fact that one realises that most players in the team are half one's age and that you are playing alongside teammates who could well be your grandson is enough of a shock to make even the most diehard player think about calling it quits. It is then that the idea of retirement becomes an obvious haven to which one must head with all speed.

The passing years generally see a move towards the middle of the field. Backs move in from the wings, first to fly half, then to the safety of the pack, starting in the second row and finally, in the twilight of the twilight, to the front row. Teeth loss and failing joints mean the injuries that can be inflicted by the opponents are greatly reduced and it is not uncommon in local league rugby to come across a front row of forty-seven year olds who can all boast of their once proud past at county standards.

What's more it is a mix that suits many clubs since the full spectrum of the age range can be accommodated on the field giving everyone from old to even older the opportunity of a game.

The one problem emerges in the old boy

teams where by nature the average age is older and no longer can a forty year old be certain of a place in the pack. In these teams the twilight player may be well past dusk in his playing career by the time he reaches the sanctuary of the pack, while the front row might accumulate enough years for their own joint bi-centenary.

The twilight season

The twilight months from May to September offer the rugby player the chance to put his feet up and, bar a possible tour, forget about rugby altogether. The fanatical few will stay in training during the lay-off months to keep fit. The remainder save any training till a frantic few days at the end of August – or not at all.

It remains then for the enthusiast to find other ways of filling his time during these twilight months. Some, indeed the majority, will content themselves with putting their feet up. But a game few will insist on other sporting releases for their energies. But what?

Remember the game of rugby is based around the twin principals of brute force and intimidation. Sports that offer the chance for a measure of both are to be preferred. Cricket is a promising choice. Rugby players make adequate fast bowlers, sacrificing line and spin for pure brute force. It is purely random whether they bowl a spectacular wide or take a spectacular wicket. At the crease they make adequate middle-order batsmen as well, especially where cavalier run-makers are required. They might be out first ball, or they might equally go on to make fifty.

Tennis too is not far from the rugby player's ideal. Not the graceful art as performed at Wimbledon though. No, the rugby player's tennis game consists of smashing the service down the court as fast as possible with the avowed intent of decapitating his opponent. If the ball is returned (and remember the second serve is identical to the first so the double fault count is high), then he will sweep at it as though his life depended on it. His favourite shot is the forearm smash and his least favourite is the delicate drop shot. In doubles he will remember his scrumming technique where gross intimidation was the order of the day and he will deliberately aim any net cord rallies at the midriff of his opponent. He will think nothing of diving full length for a return (even on hardcourts) and will be marked out by his outfit which consists of rugby gear with trainers.

Bowls is less promising. Here the rugby player's skill will have little chance to flower and his one trump card will be the blitzkrieg shot fired with full force across the green with the aim of taking out the jack and as many of the other balls as possible. A game of bowls with a rugger player resembles less the gentle art of strategy and more a re-enactment of the Battle of the Midway.

Badminton offers even less. Brute force is met by a stubbornness of the shuttlecock to respond and guile and cunning count for more than any brutish haymaker. It is a toss up whether the rugby player damages himself or the net first and either way he is unlikely to stick at it for long.

Athletics offers a passable alternative. Especially in the field sports where brute force comes back into play. While swimming, sailing and water sports accommodate some brutishness quite readily.

But the only other sport where the rugger player can really let rip with all his regular venom is on the golf links. Again wild, misplaced violence does not guarantee a low handicap but at least the rugger player can see some return for his vengeance, even if it is only in the form of shattered clubhouse windows and divots the size of aircraft hangars.

The rugby player will address his game with verve and enthusiasm and will see more rough than a trip through the red light district of Amsterdam.

But he will enjoy it and apart from a bill in lost golf balls that rivals the national debt, he will be rewarded with a pleasant summer till it is time to return to the rugger field again.

Magazines

The following is a selection of magazines that provide useful additional rugby reading for the keen fan:

Rugby Stamp Collector

With a circulation of seven copies, this is *the* acknowledged leader in the field of philately and rugby. Recent articles have included articles on why there are no stamps devoted to English rugby, why there are no stamps devoted to Scottish rugby, and why there are no stamps devoted to Welsh rugby.

Gay (Rugby) News
(incorporating *Bugger Rugger Monthly*)

Specialist publication especially for the gay rugby player, that has merged with its sister (or is it brother) paper to provide a fascinating one and a half page insight into the entire gay rugby scene.

WHICH Jock Strap?

Latest in the long list of Consumer Association publications; tri-annual, it is the voice of the jock strap consumer.

The town of Rugby

Rugby must be unique in that it is one of very few sports to have a town named after it. There is, for instance, no town of 'Football' or 'Tennis' or 'Cricket' or 'Ice hockey', or 'Synchronised swimming' – at least not as far as I know.

This firmly, and indeed literally, places rugby on the map of the world.

Unfortunately, this honour is mollified somewhat by a closer inspection of the town itself. For Rugby shares a rare, peculiar distinction, together with many other of the dreary towns of Middle England (Corby, Kettering, Nuneaton, Northampton, Leighton Buzzard, Milton Keynes, Daventry and the like) in that it sparks off absolutely nothing in the imagination.

No famous song has ever been written about Rugby. Nor is it immortalised in play, or film. ('Rugby, Rugby' is not a hard-hitting drama filmed by Martin Scorsese; 'From Rugby With Love' is not an action-packed Bond drama starring Roger Moore; 'The Rugby Connection' is not the long-awaited sequel to the successful French Connection movies.) And to my knowledge no great masterpiece has ever been put on canvas as a result of the inspiration of the town of Rugby.

In short, Rugby is known for practically nothing – other than rugby. Apart from the dubious distinction of being the first stop after Watford Junction on most Inter City journeys out of London, Rugby does have the minor honour of sharing its name with the one plastered on the garish orange side of half the concrete mixers in this country. Neither of these shared triumphs, alas, could be considered a great or lasting claim to fame for the town.

Few famous people have come from Rugby. Nor have many visited. Unless it was speeding through on an Inter City 125 on their way elsewhere. Nor is Rugby the famous world centre for any trade or profession, unless you include concrete manufacture, which is in itself one of the duller trades one might care to consider.

No, with all frankness, Rugby is not a town that has left its mark. A minor blemish perhaps. Or a slightly unpleasant stain. Or a difficult-to-remove splodge. But not a mark.

So let us salute that town that shares its name with the long ball game. But, frankly, unless you are very keen, I wouldn't bother to actually go there.

Marriage – to have and to hold off

Many instances of players being married before an important game and missing the reception to take part in the match have been recorded. Many more instances of best men rushing from the church to make a crunch fixture are recorded. Or of groom and groom's friends slipping off unnoticed at the reception to dash to the ground and cheer on their country.

But there is only one recorded case of a husband and wife actually being joined together in matrimony, on the pitch, while a game was in progress. And that concerns Desmond and Edna Punt, of Doncaster, in 1973.

Desmond was a keen local player, and when it was learnt that his marriage would coincide with a vital league fixture he took the unusual step of killing two birds with one stone. Approaching the club secretary and explaining his dilemma he was reassured to know that his bride, best man, and the clergyman might all be made honorary team mem-

bers and might take the field at three o'clock with the rest of the team.

The procedure was then quite simple. Wife, best man and vicar merely had to keep up with play as the service was read through the vicar's loudhailer. Vows were exchanged in a line-out, the ring passed over in a scrum, and the first kiss shared on the goalline while waiting for the opponents to make a conversion.

Indeed the whole ceremony ran far more smoothly than anyone had envisaged. There was an awkward moment early on when the bride, in ivory, received the ball in a flowing move and was floored with a thundering tackle from which she took several minutes to recover. And there was another moment later on when the vicar was trying to read his sermon only to be bundled into touch and dumped over an advertising hoarding.

But the eventual result was a novel and memorable occasion. Bride and groom hopped into the tub with the rest of the players after the match for a rub and scrub while the vicar entered into the spirit and swapped shirts with the opponents' fullback.

The other players all acted as witnesses to the ceremony while both families watched from the stands. A nice touch came when the bride, as is traditional, threw her bouquet of flowers to the bridesmaids, only for the opponents' lock forward to dash in and catch them, run fully fifty yards down the touchline, and ground them behind the posts claiming a try. (Which, on protest, was given.)

(There is no recorded instance of a player giving birth during a game!)

15

FURTHER APPENDIX

Rugby Book of Records

Longest time to take a conversion

Took place in a game between South Wickingham and St Brandan's Third Fifteen. The South Wickingham captain elected to take the kick himself and found he was kicking into a stiff headwind. Despite several attempts, the ball rolled back on each run up. A second player was elected to hold the ball but by this time the wind had picked up to gale force and at the vital moment a sudden gust of wind blew the ball away again. With the wind speed gusting to force twelve a third player was elected to join the second in holding the ball down. Again this proved insufficient and eventually after some 25 minutes' organisation the kick was made with eight players surrounding the ball to secure it in place and to act as a human windshield. The kick itself was fluffed and rolled forward three inches whereupon a re-kick was awarded and the match abandoned.

Most players in one jock strap

This is held by five members of the Royal Merchant Navy team who successfully shared the same jock strap for 30 seconds, the minimum amount of time required for the record to stand. Players considering this record are warned only to attempt it if there is full medical back up present as a number of unpleasant and unnecessary accidents have befallen would-be record holders.

Most jock straps on one player

Edward Fitzhammel Peters is the official record holder with 87 jock straps attached to his loins on 23 June 1984 in the club bar of the North by North West Ealing club. An official attempt was made to beat the record in 1987 when a Turkish rugby player claimed to have worn 137 jock straps in a bottom of division match. This record has never been collaborated although an inconclusive photograph was published in the *Turkish Rugby Revue* and later in the Turkish edition of *Bondage International*.

Most sexually exciting position in a rugby team

The positions on the rugby field are not the same as positions in the bedchamber and there are few rugger positions that can be said to be truly erogenous. In fact it is hard to find a single rugby position that is even mildly stimulating. This is why eighty minutes of rugger are often considered to be one of the best and most successful contraceptives available. If a choice had to be made then lock forward would probably be most people's choice as the sexiest, although few people can explain why.

Most dangerous plunge bath

The visitors' plunge bath at the El Cossa club in Brazil is commonly agreed to be the most dangerous. As well as a swarm of piranhas, the bath has several sea snakes and a rare man-eating sharkfish. Few players take the plunge, fewer still survive. Visiting teams have consistently complained to the President and Captain of the club but they have refused all approaches to change the bath, claiming the fish save on heating bills (anyone who bothers with the bath is in hot enough water already and clearly has other worries beside the temperature) and on water rates (there is no point changing the water after a game since so few players bathe in it).

Muddiest player ever on a rugby pitch

Many muddy players have graced the rugby field but none so muddy as Byron Elsemere, a prop in the lower division of the Shropshire League between the wars. He seemed unable to enjoy himself unless he was muddy and regarded the mudbath as the compulsory adjunct to any game. Never happier was he than when dripping with the stuff and black from head to toe. So desperate was he to become muddy in his later years that he would contrive situations where he could become muddy when none offered themselves. He would suddenly roll or dribble the ball forward into a muddy patch and dive after it when there was no player for fifty yards. Or he would collect the ball direct from the kick off, ignore his fellow team members and dart to a sticky patch near the touchline and dive in headfirst. At the bitter end he even took to running from the field and burying himself in a duckpond in the adjoining field or dunking himself in a water meadow two miles away several hours before the game began.

Unluckiest try attempt ever

This record belongs to Carl Grosvenor of Frimble 'B' in a junior league match on 23 March 1952. Grosvenor took the ball and seemed to be heading for an easy try when a late tackle caused him to barge into the posts. Although he continued his progress between the posts the collision had unseated the uprights' foundations. The result was that as he went under for his try the posts swung down and the left-hand leg hooked his shirt end before coming to rest at a drunken 45 degree angle to the pitch. Grosvenor was thus left dangling six feet above the ground unable to touch the ball down yet out of reach of his opponents. He was left to hang there for twenty minutes until the final whistle, ending up loser on the pitch, but winner of the most unlucky try attempt record.

Most thespian line judge

Must certainly go to Brett Walker, a line judge in the Southern Counties division. A failed actor, Brett lives out his fantasies on the rugby field. Some decisions take up to five minutes to unravel, such is his acting prowess. Indeed on one occasion he rolled in agony for over half an hour moaning the death scene from Hamlet and clutching at his chest and heart, simply to indicate a forward pass.

Most violent rugby player in history

This dubious honour probably goes to Lewis Jones who played in the Porthcawl region in the early sixties. He was known as the wild man of rugby and was indiscriminating in his violence. He would emerge from the changing room spoiling for a fight and would likely as not have picked one before the game had started. He rarely lasted longer than five minutes and one season never made it even as far as the start. Even when he was sent off the violence wouldn't abate. He would abuse fans and officials alike and would even have a tussle with the tea lady if she rose to the bait. When he couldn't provoke a fight, he would end up beating himself up to satisfy his insatiable lust for violence, and many a game has been punctuated by the bizarre and somewhat distasteful sight of Jones, on the touchline, headbutting himself, to the roars of the fans.

Most trivial reason for cancelling a match

This honour goes to Arnold Prescott, referee in a Swimbourne versus South Leicester match in December 1971. With both teams on the pitch and warming up, he decided to cancel the match because he didn't really feel like it. Two years later he was in trouble again for cancelling another game on a whim after ten minutes' play, and later that year for halting another game just to 'see what would happen' if he did. He still referees a few major games (if he feels like it).

Ripley's Book of Facts

Handing on the gum shield at Biddleshum Old Boys

Biddleshum School was founded in 1843 by Sir Henry Biddleshum, a noted philanthropist and pioneer of the lease-hire pit pony. The school was completed after his death and has long boasted a first, second and colts' fifteen. The Old Boys first took to the field in 1879 and in 1886 joined the West Sussex League. Which was odd as the school was in Northumberland. For many years the Old Boys have enjoyed the tradition of handing on the gum shield. This is the gum shield of the first captain, William T Escott, who was killed tragically in an early battle of the First World War (so early it took place in 1911). Since that time the gum shield has been handed down to successive captains and worn by them as a mark of respect. When a new captain is picked, the gum shield is ceremoniously passed on in a cut glass goblet on an ermine trimmed cushion. By tradition the gum shield must never be washed nor shall it be cleansed in any way. The tradition lives on to this day.

The kamikaze prop forwards of the Japanese Combined Forces' rugby team

Players playing against the Japanese Combined Forces' team have long experienced this strange and unnerving phenomenon. Japanese Air Force representatives, trained in the ancient art of ritual suicide by hara-kiri will often throw themselves on to their swords after a poor or undistinguished performance. Even a missed drop goal from fifty yards has been followed by the player running from the field to disembowel himself as a mark of shame. Officials have done much to discourage the custom over recent years and have suggested other less drastic action in the form of extra training, but their influence has at best been moderate. The problem isn't simply the dampening of spirits that mass suicide can bring to post-match frolics, nor the trauma of knowing that should you score a winning try you might consign your opponents to death. It is more the practical problem that mass death can have on team selection. Losing half your squad to injury can be bad enough but when you lose half of them to the sword after every defeat, then team selection really does become difficult. Equally difficult is the task of building up a settled squad. No sooner has a team started to mould together as a unit than they have a slight hiccup, lose a game, and all rush off to kill themselves.

Rugby on the moon

When Edwin 'Buzz' Aldrin landed on the moon and took out his golf clubs, it signalled the arrival of golf as the sport of the world. After all it was the first sport to gain footage in outer space. Yet few of us realise how strong and how hard the rugby lobby campaigned to have a rugby ball taken aboard the same spacecraft. The rugby supporters argued their case on the simple grounds that golf was elitist and not representative of the world's people, whereas rugby was the true sport of egality. They also argued that a rugby ball was cheaper than a golf club and that since the mission was costing so much every penny saved was to be applauded. And they further argued that if there was a problem they would themselves provide the ball free of charge just to make sure that NASA didn't have to cough up. Unfortunately, despite all this, golf won the day but considerable correspondence took place between the rugby authorities and the Kennedy Space Centre over the 'rugby crisis' and even up to a few days before lift-off Buzz Aldrin was being fitted with a special lunar rugby kit. This kit is now on show at the NASA Space Museum in a locked room (please apply in advance for permission to view).

The El Quito Rugby Club of Bolivia

There is only one rugby club in Bolivia: the El Quito Rugby Union Club – where the lack of opponents has meant the team are undefeated in over forty years and in the last thirty-six years haven't conceded a point. They haven't actually scored one either, but no matter. It is a record the players and officials of the club are rightly proud of and are keen to preserve. Approaches to play a game by visiting teams are turned down flat. Tours abroad are not even considered. The President of the club has hired a militia of local gunmen to guard the pitch and ensure no match ever takes place, and the post of fixtures secretary has been left vacant for thirty-eight years after the previous four occupants all died in mysterious circumstances in a period of a few months. Two years ago an uprising by younger players who wished to start playing again took place with the attempted overthrow of the committee, but the revolt was put down amid fierce fighting and much bloodshed. Visiting rugby teams are advised to avoid the club at all times lest they be shot.

The lone flyhalf of Loch MacCready

Few people visit Loch MacCready, least hospitable of the Scottish glens. The landscape is barren, the lake itself featureless and a freak of the landscape causes an icy wind to blow down the lake on even the most pleasant day. Yet it is here that Angus Drachona has decided to spend his days, alone with the elements. Alone to pace the loch shores, teeing up an ageing rugby ball and spot kicking it along the shore edge in a never-ending trek around the lake. This dutiful act is one of penance for a simple missed conversion when Angus played for West of Scotland 'B'. So mortified was Angus by his mistake that he took himself off to Loch MacCready, there to spend the rest of his days in solitary penance, kicking a rugby ball round and round so he might never forget the wicked evil he had done. No-one ever approaches Angus nor asks him his thoughts. He is locked away with his bitterness and asks only to be left in peace. In 1983, with a stiff wind blowing he drove his ball into the loch and very nearly drowned retrieving it. Since that day he has worn a life-belt and waterwings in readiness. If you see a lone Scotsman in rugby kit and waterwings kicking a threadbare ball round a loch in Scotland then chances are it is Angus.

Safe rugby

Safe rugby is very similar to safe sex. To enjoy safe rugby you should remember the following points:

1 The safest way to practise safe rugby is to not play rugby at all. If this is not possible, then try and reduce the number of people you come into contact with on the rugby field.
2 You can't catch rugby from a toilet seat.
3 In some third world countries, such as Wales, as many as sixty per cent of the population carry an enthusiasm for the game of rugby and have been diagnosed rugby positive.

4 Never share a jock strap. Sharing a jock strap is one of the commonest ways that a person may catch the rugby bug. (And several other things as well.)
5 Contrary to public belief, there is no truth in the myth that you can catch rugby from Bill McLaren.
6 Contact your doctor if you notice any of the following symptoms: wild desire to run around a mudpatch; unexplained bouts of spontaneous drinking and singing; halucinations and/or daydreams of playing rugby for England; a sudden interest in 'Rugby Special' on BBC 2.

Ruggergrams

Ruggergrams have been in existence now for quite some time and offer a genuine alternative to the normal forms of telegram greeting service. Ruggergrams come in three sizes (15 stone, 18 stone and 21 stone) and in a wide variety of club kits. The Ruggergram himself will knock on your door, leap on top of the victim and claim that he or she hasn't released the ball. He will continue to grapple with his victim until physically restrained by those around him.

Ruggergrams are ideal for birthdays, parties, or any occasion in honour of someone you don't like. Costs are reasonable (£25.00 plus beer money [average £75.00]) but do not include full medical insurance cover (£300) or breakages, and Ruggergrams are keen to point out that they are not liable for death or injury arising from any greeting.

One popular use for a Ruggergram is during a real game of rugby where the Ruggergram will suddenly tackle the victim at the same time that the legitimate tackler is grabbing his ankle in the other direction.

Ruggerstrippergrams are also available and operate on much the same principal as the normal Ruggergram except the player removes his clothes before making the tackle. Again they may be used in a conventional game of rugby.

Strippingruggernunsograms work on the same principal as above except the player wears a nun's frock over his rugby gear and sings two verses from the nuns' chorus in 'The Sound of Music' before making his tackle. Only available in the 21-stone version.

Booklist

In compiling this book I have been assisted by a number of texts. Among those providing useful guidance and inspiration were:

Chairman Mao's Little Red Hook
Based on the original *Little Red Book,* in this further work Mao lays down the communist theories on rugby football for the Chinese people.

Country Diary of an Edwardian Lady Rugby Player
Disastrous marketing exercise in which the publishing sensation of the eighties was adapted for a male market. Same style as the original text but with rugby providing the focal point for the artwork and text.

The Reader's Digest Book of the Gum Shield
450 lavishly hand-tooled pages with over a thousand full colour illustrations. £92.

A La Recherche Du Temps Perdu by Marcel Proust (with an introduction by Bill Beaumont)
This new edition contains a frank and earnest introduction by former England captain Bill Beaumont in which he discusses his England career and the evolution of the modern international game.

It Came From Hull Kingston Rovers
The story of a hideously deformed alien creature that came to Hull and was selected for the Hull front line without anyone noticing.

The Concise Dictionary of Rugby English
Contains the full dictionary of rugby English (all eight words).

Rosslyn Park Wives
Jackie Collins's much awaited sequel to *Hollywood Wives* in which she rips the lid off the stormy lifestyle of the glam and glitzy Rosslyn Park second extra 'B' team's better halves.

Peter Wright's Rugby Tactics
Peter Wright's latest attempt to gain publicity is this gratuitous tactics manual in which he describes scrum technique through his experiences as a former member of MI5.

Superstars

The twilight years of my career were brightened by the emergence of the 'Superstars' series on TV. The concept of the series was in the true ideal of amateur sport, namely sportsmen competing in sports in which they were not proficient (in the case of British women's tennis this would allow them the unique advantage of taking part in their own sport). However, like all ideals, it was shaky to uphold. For a start, certain sports clearly produce all-round sportsmen well able to turn their hands, and feet, to other pursuits. While others, alas, do not. It does not take a superbrain to work out that Sebastian Coe is likely to beat the socks off Jocky Wilson in most sports going, while Bill Werbenuik is hardly going to provide stiff opposition to Daley Thompson, no matter what the sport.

At the same time, while the competition works on the unitarian basis that everyone takes part in everyone else's sport bar their own, there are certain obvious anomalies to this rule. Ski-jumping, for instance, is one sport which has not to my knowledge figured on the programme despite the presence of ski-jumpers in the contest. Nor has sumo wrestling, Cumberland wrestling, or bull-fighting ever featured. Players from these sports are therefore at a distinct disadvantage in the contest.

In an effort to spread the appreciation of the Superstars ideal I have devised a simple 'home version'. Basically the rules are as the televised version but the actual sports have been narrowed down.

Six sports for home Superstars:
1 Subbuteo
2 Tiddlywinks
3 Kerplunk
4 Ping pong
5 Blow football
6 Bagatelle

Other alternatives:
Hunt the thimble
Musical chairs
Off Ground Tig
Scalelectrix

Useful addresses

Readers of this book may find the following addresses of use:

Aerolines Argentinas
c/o Heathrow Airport
London
(when a hasty retreat is required)

St Bartholomews's Hospital
Casualty Department
West Smithfield Rd
London EC1

Guinness Book of Records
Guinness Superlatives Ltd
33 London Road
Enfield
(address your letter to the Rugby and Bodily Disfigurement Editor)

Jim'll Fix It
BBC TV Centre
Wood Lane
London W12 8QT

Pope John Paul II
c/o Vatican City
nr Rome
Italy
(please mark your envelope 'Personal')

Scotland Yard
Serious Crimes Squad
New Scotland Yard

The Fish Marketing Board
c/o Billingsgate Fish Market
London E14
(Not immediately useful but you never know when these things might come in handy, do you?)

The Samaritans
(Branches in most towns, check Yellow Pages under 'The Samaritans'; will answer questions about personal and emotional problems. Not specifically equipped to answer questions about rugby but may be able to help out with general answers.)